MARIA D' ANDREA'S SECRET OCCULT GALLERY AND SPELL CASTING FORMULARY

A Psychic Insider's Personal Study Guide To Over 50 Rarely Discussed Occult Topics – Plus Maria's Most Powerful Spells Never Revealed Previously!

Maria D' Andrea

Maria D' Andrea's
SECRET OCCULT GALLERY
AND SPELL CASTING FORMULARY

By Maria D'Andrea, MsD, D.D., DRH

Copyright ©2003 & 2012 by Maria D' Andrea

All Rights Reserved

No part of this book may be reproduced, stored in a retrieval system, in any form or by any means, electronic, photocopying, recording, or otherwise, without prior permission of the author and publisher.

ISBN 13: 9781606111284
ISBN 10: 1606111280

Special thanks to Maria E. Berde, my mother, for her endless energy and effort which she used to transfer this collection to an electronic format for me. Her own experience as a published writer has contributed to the layout of this collection without measure.

Timothy Green Beckley, Publisher
Inner Light Publications/Global Communications
For Our Free Weekly Newsletter And
Mail Order Catalog Go To:
www.ConspiracyJournal.com
www.TeslaSecretLab.com
Write Or Telephone: 732 602-3407
Tim Beckley – Inner Light
Box 753, New Brunswick, NJ 08903

SECRET OCCULT GALLERY AND SPELL CASTING FORMULARY

By Maria D'Andrea, MsD, D.D., DRH

CONTENTS

Dedication viii
Why This Occult Gallery Is Important To You ix
Introduction x
Psychic Self-Defense 1
The Concept Of Herbs Related To The Occult 2
Energy Streams: Mother Nature's Party Lines 4
Are You A Modern Day Prophet? 6
Children In the Path of Light 8
Manifesting Your Own Future 12
The Outlook of a Mystic 15
Power of Belief 18
Communication On A Psychic Level 22
Guided By The Spiritual Realm 25
The Secret Power Within Crystals and Candles 28
Journey To Another Plane 30
Earth Changes And How They Affect You 34
Stones Of Intrigue 36
Alpha Reality 38
U.F.O's And Crystals 40

Colored Lights - How Your Exposure To Them Can Affect You	50
Wind Magick	52
Choices On Your Path	54
The Call To Ministry	56
U.F.O.'s On The Astral Plane	58
Forms With Power	62
Lucid Dreams	64
Ghost Versus Spirit	67
Sounds Of Power	69
Symbolic Magick	71
My Invisible Partner	73
Imagination Versus Psychic	76
The Friendly Visitor	78
Prosperity And Happiness Are All Yours	80
When You Are Guided By Spiritual Beings	80
Healing: God's Natural Way To Perfect Harmony	81
The Out-Of-Body Experience: How To Travel Without Luggage	83
Telepathy: Direct Communication	85
Ghostology: Finding Unseen Forces	88
The Inner Kingdom	90
New Age Formulary	92
The UFO Investigator	94
Hobgoblins	98
Ghosts Of The Tribes	100
The Tidra	102

The Link Between Realities	105
Story Of The Bats	107
Story About Earth: How Did the Earth Become A Brilliant Star?	112
Empowerment Through The Word	114
Influence Of UFO's On Spiritual Awareness	116
Voodoo Dolls: Ancient Tools For Modern Man	118
We Are The Law Of Abundance Manifest	120
Dreams: Your Direct Phone Line	122
Dream Pillows	126
God's Creatures – A Psychic Connection	128
Psychic Rune Casting To American Indian Crafts	130
Universal Lines of Force	132
Tree Doctor	133
Conclusion	136
About The Author	137
Notes	138
Other Books, Services And Products	139

DEDICATION

To Howard, whose technical and creative side shows a special blend of spirituality.

To my son, Rob D'Andrea, who is on his own spiritual quest. He makes life an adventure.

To my son, Rick Holecek and his wife Gina, whose energies elevate those around them with their positive outlooks.

To my mother, Maria Berde for her writing abilities. She keeps things lively with Mother Nature.

To my spiritual brother, Bro. Francis E. Revels-Bey, for creatively living and bringing forth the spirit of Divine Grace.

To Howard Solomon, whose technical and creative side helped complete this book.

To Timothy Beckley, who enables me to live up to my Higher Self and is a great friend.

WHY THIS OCCULT GALLERY IS IMPORTANT TO YOU

The author of this collection, having a Doctorate in Religious Humanities and a Doctorate in Metaphysics, as well as receiving other degrees and certificates, has a wealth of knowledge in all of these subjects.

She was asked to write these articles for various magazines and publications and she felt that, although the pieces were short because of the available space, they will nevertheless help readers to satisfy their interest in certain subjects. She gives basic introductions and explanations in each area, so that all of you will be able to have a choice.

When interested in a specific topic, you may then avail yourselves of her books to study the details. You can also attend some of her lectures, seminars, and workshops or get in touch with her by calling her to discuss matters of interests to you. As you, the readers, leaf through this collection, you will feel closer to God, experience peace and gain precious knowledge. So, go ahead, start to explore and realize how you can be a part of ***THE OCCULT GALLERY.***

Maria E. Berde, Teacher, Librarian

INTRODUCTION

Through the numerous articles I have written and my last three books, I will aid you in a clearer understanding of the world around us, both the seen and the unseen.

We are meant to deal from both realities: the physical and the spiritual. I always tell my clients and students that it is difficult to be only spiritual, since you would starve without the physical. If you try to deal ONLY with the physical, you will again be out of balance. You need to work with both. This book deals with various aspects of the spiritual realm, mainly serious levels to aid in your upward climb on the spiritual ladder and some geared more towards the young.

When working from a magick level, it is not only magick. Working with and through nature entails numerous levels of knowledge including: alchemy, colors, numerology, astrology, astronomy, physics, cycles in nature, plants, energy streams, charkas, chi and psychic abilities.

Work on the positive side in all things and you will be amazed at how fast you will progress.

Your health will pick up, your finances, relationships, business and every aspect of your life.

We all have psychic and metaphysical abilities. Practice these and they will automatically snowball and heighten. Utilize the methods in this book. Do not just read them.

Remember, you can exert control to change your life now and make your dreams and desires reality!

Maria D'Andrea's Secret Occult Gallery And Spell Casting Formulary

Psychic Self-Defense

Anytime you work with spirit, you need to know how to protect yourself.

Always use a shield before you start dealing with anything on a psychic level; you are too open otherwise. You need psychic defense for various reasons. A psychic attack is the conscious or intentional sending of negative vibrations or thoughts from one or more persons to another. Some who will be helped by this are: mystics, psychics, occultists, business people (from rivals), and nurses. You need to fortify your aura, the energy field which surrounds your physical and astral body.

To put up your shield, you need to do the following, which is the strongest:

You should relax physically – picture yourself in the center of a white egg shape. Visualize it as starting a foot below your feet up to a foot above your head. You can start at either end. Now say: "I am now putting up God's Shield of White Light of Love, Truth and Protection. Nothing negative or harmful can get in, only positive and good."

You are now protected from negativity but you are open to positive opportunity. This will shield you from negative spirit and tone down negativity from other people. The White Light will flow through your body and its vibration will strengthen your aura. You need to know this light will always be with you.

Visualize this for a few minutes. After a while you will be able to put it up extremely fast. Notice how at peace you feel within this light. You can always have this feeling anytime or place. You only need to practice.

Maria D'Andrea's Secret Occult Gallery And Spell Casting Formulary

The Concept Of Herbs Related To The Occult

There are those who say herbs that are used for occult reasons are evil, only for harm and destruction. Though opinions often differ on any matter of value, you must admit an herb does not have any control over the use it is put to, only the person using it. Many misconstrue the meaning of the occult and thus confuse the issue.

It is only that which is considered mysterious, supernatural, the unknown. With the right knowledge it can do wonders ...

As an example: there are sixteen magickal plants of power, written of by the well-acknowledged Albertus Magnus. He also included the time, season, appropriate way for picking the herbs and their uses. Some are to some extent medicinal, while some attract love, money, power, control and serve numerous other purposes.

Herbs, roots and bark have been employed since ancient times by Druids, Romans, Egyptians and diverse unknown cultures, as well as by priests and sorcerers down through the ages. The Knowledge has been passed down through sects and persons of power.

There exist a number of books available on medical or medicinal herbal uses. Most will say not to use them instead of a physician. There are also a number of books for the occult use that let you know what to mix them with and for what purpose. Authors of occult and other books do not always give the same uses for an herb; however that is only due to its versatility. Mainly in dealing with the occult, herbs are utilized to cast spells. They vibrate to certain planets, angels, days and hours.

Maria D'Andrea's Secret Occult Gallery
And Spell Casting Formulary

At times they are used as extracts, in teas, used in baths, worn as a talisman, buried, sprinkled and thrown to the winds. They are used as needed for divergent purposes such as: protecting or hexing, to make wishes come true, to attract or hold love, money, power or control. Any intention you may conceive can be helped one way or another with an herb.

Some of the most well known are chamomile, mugwort, comfrey, vervaine and nettle.

Chamomile, for instance, may be incorporated in various ways:

Externally:

Skin – for wrinkles and facial steaming hair – for blond highlights as a rinse for softness

Eyes – Compress

Bath – Soothing

Pain – As poultice

Internally:

Sleep – Tea, tonic

Appetite – Improves

Aids weak stomach and for nervous diseases

Occult:

Gambling – (especially cards) – wash hands in brew for luck ahead of time

Love – Mix with lavender and put into your clothes drawer

Herbs, though not necessarily understood by all, have been so employed for thousands of centuries. Nothing that stays with us such a length of time can be said to not work when properly used or to be only harmful. The more regard we pay towards our pasts, the more we may control and enliven our futures.

**Maria D'Andrea's Secret Occult Gallery
And Spell Casting Formulary**

Energy Streams: Mother Nature's Party Lines

The Energy Currents have been utilized for centuries by Magi, High Priests, Priestesses, and others of higher awareness levels.

These energy streams, rivers and waves are invisible forces that flow over and under the earth surfaces. Think of them as a network of crossing lines of energy, spaced at varied intervals. They are fixed and thus over the centuries will remain in the same place.

When these streams of Mother Earth are felt or seen psychically, they would appear much as a grid fixed in space.

The energy streams are a natural part of the environment.

Inasmuch as they are always there, though unseen physically, we are able to find them. There are several methods. One such method is a dowsing rod specifically programmed for this purpose by a dowser. Another way is to have a psychic or someone sensitive to these energies look for them.

These currents have more of an influence in our lives than people realize. They are positive energy lines and have several effects that are known to us as occultists.

Their vibrations affect plant life, animals, sea life and us.

They can cause mood, attitude, mental and health changes, depending on where you are located.

As an example: a person living in a house located within an energy stream would have a more positive attitude, be healthier and have more of a happy, joyous character. While this same person, having never lived in the currents, would be more depressed, could be a criminal or have ill health or what some term as bad luck.

In these days of more mobility and easier travel, we are not as stationary and the effects may not be as noticed or as influential.

However, if you are aware, as an example, that you are not in an energy stream in the place you rented for your business and it is not working well at all, you can change locations, thus improving your business. Have you ever noticed how there may be one store that has a constant change of owners over a short span of years, each owner selling various products that did not work out? Yet, the location could be on a busy street. Logically, not all the products could be non-profitable, yet when these same people relocate, their business improves.

These waves are also considered a doorway. Many paranormal occurrences and UFO sightings are within these waves. UFOs are seen in some areas more frequently than other areas. These locations have the earth's streams. There are many aspects of nature used by the magi and High priestesses consciously, this being one of many.

The more aware you are about the environment and what is going on around you, the more you can work with the Law of Nature to improve your life. Work on always being positive, improving your life and staying on the Path of Light.

**Maria D'Andrea's Secret Occult Gallery
And Spell Casting Formulary**

Are You A Modern Day Prophet?

"Prophecy" is an ancient Greek word meaning psychic message. Prophecy at that point in time concerned mainly psychic information on the country or its leaders and was thought to be sent from God.

Nowadays, prophecy includes any psychic information concerning the future on a large scale. It is information of the future on a grand scale as opposed to information concerning individuals.

Prophecy comes true because it involves group Karma and too many individuals would have to change in order to divert the Karma already set into motion.

Economic conditions affect the nation and for this reason there are professional prophets hired by governments. You may have read in the newspaper about people who predicted earthquakes or of those who had prior knowledge of floods or varied earth changes. Some predicted the assassination of President John F. Kennedy. There were those who knew exactly what would happen and tried to warn him. Julius Caesar consulted with a prophet on a regular basis, as did many leaders and prominent figures in history and in present times as well. What about Nancy Regan and her astrologer?

In our time, there is an open attitude toward Psychic Phenomenon. There are numerous books referring to prophets and the best is the Bible. John the Baptist, although he was not "The Prophet," meaning the one who was to announce the coming of the Messiah, was receiving prophetic messages (John 1). The prophet Micaiah warned King Ahab of Israel there would be impending disaster if he attacked Ramoth (2nd Chronicles 18: 2 –27). Micaiah was not heeded, thus the King died.

Maria D'Andrea's Secret Occult Gallery
And Spell Casting Formulary

You can develop your own prophetic ability. Take notes when you get a strong first impression of anything on a large scale. Be aware of how you feel at the time and write down even those things you do not understand, like a strange symbol, math sequence, etc. Information comes to us in varied forms. Review your notes after a few weeks. Have you read or saw or heard anything in the news that concerns your information?

Prophecy has always been with us. It is God-inspired knowledge. Prophecy is just as prevalent today as it was long ago and <u>you</u> may be one of the prophets of your age!

**Maria D'Andrea's Secret Occult Gallery
And Spell Casting Formulary**

Children In The Path Of Light

There are many children walking the Path; many aware that they are doing so, many just accepting this as their way of life.

It is important to teach the Truth from the very first.

This does not mean that you have to sit down with them and teach philosophy. What it does mean is that, as each diverse opportunity of life manifests, we have to be able to pass on the knowledge of how to handle them in the correct way. We teach by discussing, but more so by doing and showing at the time how to deal with varied situations.

Children have a natural ability to see things as they are. They will follow their first intuitive leads if allowed to do so. They will have an awareness, knowing that when they really want something positive to happen, it will come to pass. If left to their own devices, they shall also "see" other planes of reality.

It is amazing how many books are written on "how to" develop psychic ability and "how to" teach the young to be more aware, when all that is required to teach them is meditation, to listen to that still voice within and leave them alone. The biggest problem is to un-teach what adults have told them. That they "do not see" things, or "what a cute imagination" ...when all along it is real.

When you are walking the Path of Light, it is as though you are on a thin line. One side is our reality, the other side has the different planes. You can see both sides equally and have only to adjust to differentiate between the two.

Both my sons, Rick and Rob, are clairvoyant and clairaudient. They always have been. The only reason it is more apparent with them than with

Maria D'Andrea's Secret Occult Gallery
And Spell Casting Formulary

other children is that I always listen to what they tell me as reality, in which case you do have to teach them to protect themselves as a precaution. Teach them to put up the shield of White Light. Do so by saying, "I am now putting up a shield of God's protective White Light of Love and Truth. Nothing can get in that is harmful or negative, only good and positive." As you say this, picture white light starting from a few inches above your head and descending in an egg shape to surround your entire body, ending a few inches below your feet. It is very important they learn this. It is very easy for a child, since they already perceive it is real.

There are numerous things that other cultures in the past have done and that I feel could still be used as beneficial to children. For example: there are small dolls that more than one culture has used. They were given to children who were told that these dolls were for when they had a worry or a problem. They would tell their problems to the dolls. It was a way to learn positive thinking and not to worry constantly. Since they had confidence in these dolls, they went out and solved their own problems. Personally, I gave my children magick rocks to be put in their rooms and not to be touched by any other person. It was used to protect them, to keep away scary things in the night. Actually, they are quartz crystals. The vibration they put out does attract protection. It is only a matter of how you explain everything. Magick rocks, when they are little, are quartz crystals when they are bigger.

The important thing to remember is to let them know they are working through Divine Power and Guidance. There will be times when they are "aware" of something that you are not. You have to bear in mind that there are experiences that cannot be explained. In our world, we reason or explain. In the psychic realm, some things you just <u>know.</u>

It is a fact and that is all there is to it. You will only get you and the child frustrated if you keep repeating "How do you know?" There will not always be a sense of time or distance. Nothing is impossible to a child, since they are not aware of limitations yet. Children do not separate the two realities. They only see the One.

Teach them the basic principles we have just covered. Continue to always guide them gradually and they will increase in spirituality. Let them be themselves: happy, positive and free spirits.

Maria D'Andrea's Secret Occult Gallery And Spell Casting Formulary

Maria D'Andrea's Secret Occult Gallery And Spell Casting Formulary

Spell 1

Love and God

Say or think my following Prayer at least twice, the first thing when you wake up and the last thing at night. (If you can, add in one more at any time. Three times is best.)
The following was given to me while channeling.

My Father, Divine Power,
Never abandons me,
As with our Ancient Family,
From the Birth of Mankind,
He grants us all our successes.

Divine Power flows through me,
Surrounds me and uplifts me,
Where my focus goes,
My Power grows.

Through wind and rain,
Through earth and fire,
I now manifest all my desires.
(Focus on what your desires are for a minute.)
Thank You Lord. So Be It!!!

Maria D'Andrea's Secret Occult Gallery And Spell Casting Formulary

Manifesting Your Own Future

Have you ever noticed how some people always have everything they want in life? Money, good relationships, success in business and in all aspects of life? While other people seem to always have things going wrong? Do you ever wish your life could improve?

Now is the time to make that very important change come about. God wants us to be happy and to prosper. He did not say: I want you to have some things but not money, etc. The Bible said in Psalm 23:1, "The Lord is my shepherd; I shall not want." And in Psalm 122:7, "Peace be within thy walls and prosperity within thy palaces." He wants us to be happy on ALL levels. How can you be happy when you do not have enough money for food? Or if you are tense or feel frustrated with the path your life is going on?

If God created man in His image, then we must have control or an ability that we are not utilizing correctly to create positivity.

The power of the Word has been known through the ages. When we make an affirmation through Divine Power, knowing it will come to pass, it will manifest. Realize that you have infinite supply through Divine Intelligence.

Anything positive or good that you want can come into your life. You have to change your outlook first. If you think "poor," that is what you will attract. If you think "rich," then that will be attracted to you. The power of the Word is very real. It influences your subconscious, your actions, as well as the astral and physical planes.

First, see in your mind what you want, in as much detail as possible. Concentrate on it. Feel it. Know in yourself that it will happen. Then say aloud

Maria D'Andrea's Secret Occult Gallery And Spell Casting Formulary

or to yourself what, to you, expresses your desire as a positive affirmation. Such as: I am God's child and He will take care of my every need.

Things to Remember

1.—<u>Through Divine Power</u> – You are saying everything comes from God.

2.—<u>In a Perfect Way</u> – What you want will happen in a positive way that does not harm others. As an example: if you see a house you love and desire that house, you will get it. If you do not say "in a perfect way," however, you may get it due to the owners being bankrupt and having to sell their home fast and at a low price. Then you may be able to afford it. On the other hand, if you say the affirmation, you might get the house because they had a better job offer at a distance. Then they would want to move. They would still sell fast and at a low price.

3.—<u>I want this or something better</u> – You want to make sure that if you cannot have the exact thing you want, you will at least get the equal. If you do not say "or something better," you might be closing off an opportunity to do better, thus putting a limit on yourself.

4.—<u>Thank God</u> – As if it has already come to pass. Matt. 7:7, "Ask and it shall be given you, seek and ye shall find, knock, and it shall be opened unto you." The Bible does not say <u>maybe</u>. It says "shall be."

This works on all levels. You might need a new job, a new or better relationship or improved health.

Words and thoughts form our lives. You have to relax and spend 15-20 minutes concentrating on what you desire each day, knowing that it will come. Matt. 9:39, "According to your faith be it unto you." In essence, what you expect from life will be what you get. Expect good. Expect prosperity.

Make yourself interested in those around you. Be happy and let others see you care. Do not dwell on your past, but think of all the good to come in your future; be receptive to God and Spiritual law. It is like being a magnet. You attract what you want and repel what you do not.

Work with the Spiritual Law. If you have a situation in your life that is negative, do not fight it. By concentrating on it, you are giving it power.

Maria D'Andrea's Secret Occult Gallery
And Spell Casting Formulary

Relax and leave it in the hands of God. It will be taken care of.

We are all part of God. You have to act in a positive way. Use the Power of the Word, knowing that you will receive what you ask for. Remember at all times: "All things what so ever ye ask in prayer, believing, ye shall receive."

Maria D'Andrea's Secret Occult Gallery And Spell Casting Formulary

The Outlook Of A Mystic

Mysticism is a way of life, a point of view from an esoteric angel.

Many people know that there is more to life than what we understand intellectually or with our senses. This seems obvious; otherwise, we would not have churches. We would not have a belief in God, Buddha or any Divinity.

The followers of this path have had the experience of an ultimate reality. This can manifest in a variety of ways.

It can be a direct knowledge of God, such as raising the Serpent Power, known as Kundalini. Through certain methods, such as Yoga and meditation, you bring the energy up through your six charkas (energy centers). These are located along your spinal column and your third eye, found in the middle of your forehead and above your head. It has potential dangers if you do not know what you are attempting. You should never try anything without knowledge or the help of someone who can show you the way.

Another way is through insight. Have you ever noticed that the first intuitive feeling, or hunch, is always right? The first feeling you get meeting someone new or trying to make a decision will be correct. If you go by your intuition, you will realize that it was the right move. If you do not listen, you will look back and realize that you should have. That knowledge came from somewhere. You did not sit down and analyze the situation. You simply "knew."

You may also have the belief without actually having a personal experience, such as a religious belief.

When you are a follower of this path of life, you understand that you

Maria D'Andrea's Secret Occult Gallery
And Spell Casting Formulary

can attain information on a higher level. You can work with Power. When you know the essence of how things work, you can put the natural forces to use. You have to be careful to only use these forces in a positive way. Due to the Laws of Karma, you will be aware that what you do, negative or positive, will come back to you. Do unto others as you would have them do unto you.

A true mystic will always be a positive person. Enlightenment brings great joy but also great responsibility. Understanding brings peace, harmony, a oneness with everything living and material. It is having a transcendental attitude. You want to help others, to share the joy. To a degree, you do share knowledge. However, you also realize the dangers of imparting all what you are aware of to those not yet ready, those who want to use it in selfish ways or to impress others. This is not to be taken lightly or as a game. It is a "knowing," a way of living your life from day to day.

You can have influence – what others call supernatural powers. The fact is, EVERYONE can. Jesus said that what He can do, we also can do.

It depends on your perspective. As an example, when Jesus walked on water. If you think of it in different terms, as levitation, you will have a different outlook on it. Basically the Bible discusses this in Matt. 14:25, as a matter of Faith.

When you live with the mystical outlook, you will also be obligated to help wherever you can, to enlighten or be of aid in a variety of ways. There is also a belief with us that the more you put out, the more you get back. It is akin to science in some ways. For every action there is a reaction.

Spirit is considered a main element of reality. If we acknowledge our own, we must therefore give serious thought to other forms of spirit. When you can accept this, then you can understand those of us that are in communication with spirits on the other side.

There is also an understanding of the physical plane and the vibrations it puts out, such as gemstones which have a three foot vibration and are mentioned in the Bible in a passage concerning which gemstones to use when making the breastplate. (Exodus 39:10).

Gemstones are used for a number of reasons. They attract varied things into your life, such as luck, love, protection, money and health, to mention a

Maria D'Andrea's Secret Occult Gallery And Spell Casting Formulary

few. Herbs are also mentioned. The uses are too numerous to be listed here.

You also learn not to judge others. "Do not judge others, so that God will not judge you." (Matt 7:1) It is not that you are going by the Bible so much as that what is in it just happens to be what you have experienced, or what you "know."

All of us, at some time or another, talk of the ancient, the old ways or of the new awareness. Actually, they are the same on many points. The "basics" will never change. It is Universal Law. However, there are those that take the old ways and modernize them. This you have to be very careful of since you need to know why the method works. Otherwise, you will change it and possibly omit a main ingredient, in which case it will not have a very potent end result. If it keeps being changed in this way, it might get so diluted as to not work at all.

A Mystic is fully aware of the power around us, and just as aware of the source: Divine Power, through which all things are possible. Prior to what manifests for you, you already say thanks to God, knowing that the result will be coming in. You need to keep in mind that you do not have any true power. Only God does, and you are merely using it. All the forces have always been with us. It is only a matter of when we are more tuned in to them. "I am the Lord and I do not change." (Malachi 3:6)

It is like looking through a kaleidoscope. You shift it slightly and you see a different view. So it is with this outlook. You merely shift your perspective slightly and you see things in a different light.

When you are a Mystic, you live by Faith, the Knowledge of Universal Laws and the Truth.

**Maria D'Andrea's Secret Occult Gallery
And Spell Casting Formulary**

Power Of Belief

Belief is what opens doors to unlimited power. As the Bible in one form or another keeps reaffirming, there is Power in the Word or Thought.

We get so tangled up in our everyday lives on a material plane that we forget to step back, to see things in the right perspective, to see that the material plane is not all there is. We need to deal with our lives from a spiritual outlook to a material one, not the other way around.

There are many strong examples of belief; we only need to look.

Fire-walking is achieved in this manner. It is considered an art, practiced as such in Africa, India and the West Indies, among other places. The fire-walker walks barefoot through a trench of burning logs or charcoal or stones. They do not need to talk themselves into this action. They know or believe they will not get hurt. That is enough to gain the desired results.

Many people utilize subliminal tapes. The tapes help one to be rid of bad habits or to better oneself. The messages are given below your threshold of awareness. In utilizing this method, you will hear varied sounds: waves, the wind or some other soothing sound. The information comes to you on the subconscious level.

You will then put this into motion due to an inner knowing, a BELIEF in what is expected of you.

Then there is the fakir. This is a member of the Muslim religious order, although this term is now loosely applied. The Hindu fakir will sit or lie on a bed of nails or practice other methods to achieve Nirvana. He KNOWS he can do this without pain. He BELIEVES.

Maria D'Andrea's Secret Occult Gallery And Spell Casting Formulary

There are many factors to be considered when you contemplate what the different beliefs are. In the end, however, what it all comes back to is that if the belief is strong, you can accomplish anything. There are no limits. What the mind can conceive can come to pass. Whatever your needs are, you can manifest them on an earth plane.

For example, if you would like to own a car, but you feel there isn't any way at this particular time in your life, then you simply will not have one. However, if you KNOW that you will have the car and you do not think of all the negative aspects, if you put your faith in Divine Power and believe, then you will acquire the car. You will not know ahead of time how to get to your goal. It does not really matter. The important part is to believe in the outcome. In this way it will manifest.

In essence, you are going from a thought form to a spiritual level and it then comes back down to a material plane.

Your belief can accomplish anything on a multi-level, whether you are putting something into motion on a physical, emotional or spiritual plane.

The main concept we have to remember is that we believe, we attract into our lives. If we believe we are always ill, we will be. If we believe we are healthy, then it is what will manifest into our lives. There is Power in Belief and if you work with it, you open doors to a limitless dimension.

Maria D'Andrea's Secret Occult Gallery And Spell Casting Formulary

Maria D'Andrea's Secret Occult Gallery And Spell Casting Formulary

Spell 2

Manifest With The God Box

Take a box (small box, tissue box, etc.) and make sure it has a top on it so it can be private.

Write all your prayers down on separate pieces of paper and put it in The God Box and forget about it.

Shake the box up once in a while and tell God "I'm waiting." (Or something equivalent.)

Things do work when you use the box. It releases worry about the outcome and the saying "Let God and Let Go" works.

When the Box gets full, burn the paper and throw it to the wind or just throw it out (outside your home) and use another Box.

A good way to start your prayer is with "Thank You for . . ."

Maria D'Andrea's Secret Occult Gallery
And Spell Casting Formulary

Communication On A Psychic Level

Many people have the ability to communicate with one another on a psychic level. There are numerous cases already on record.

The ones we have heard of are usually extreme, such as how a parent will "hear" a child cry out for help at a time when the child is in trouble. Then the parent gets the help there in time. The child, being at a distance, could not have actually been heard in the normal sense. This type of hearing is known as clairaudience.

Have you ever answered someone's question and then realized that they have not said anything? Or, after your answer, the person says: "I just was going to ask you about that!" That is one form of psychic communication.

There are varied ways of communication on this level, some of which we are not aware of as psychic. At times, people do not recognize what they are doing as psychic phenomenon.

First impressions are a form of this. They are correct 100% of the time. It is only a matter of listening to your first intuitive feeling or hunch. The more you direct your life by it, the more frequent the feeling becomes. It has a snowball effect. There are numerous valid reasons to listen to your first impressions.

Such as in the instance of meeting someone as a potential relationship or friendship. The person may be very warm and friendly, but if nonetheless you do not like the person, there is a reason. Later, you will find that you will not get along on some level. Instead of trying harder to be friends, more out of guilt than any other reason, do not bother to work on the friendship. There are underlying reasons for the feeling. This is probably a per-

Maria D'Andrea's Secret Occult Gallery
And Spell Casting Formulary

son who will act as a friend, and the first time you have a problem this friend will be gone. Also in reverse, such as getting a positive feeling about someone that outwardly seems negative. Learn to listen to your feelings more.

You may have a significant decision to make. Concentrate for five minutes on the decision. Look at all the aspects, both negative and positive. Do not think of anything negative and do not think of anything related to the decision after that time. Then after the given time, think of the decision once again. The first feeling you receive will be your answer.

For example, if you are considering whether to move to Florida or Alaska, if your first feeling is one of warmth or palm trees, obviously you were not meant to be in Alaska.

The majority of people assume that there are only a few ways to receive psychic information. Thus, they miss their own abilities. They ignore the input they receive. A number of theories are recognized concerning varied psychic levels. One is that, in effect, we are all born with the ability and it manifests in different forms or levels. Such as previously mentioned, people will intellectualize and try to understand. However, they do not do the most important step, which is to apply it to themselves.

This source of information is for everyone. It comes to us from the astral plane. When we need information, we tune into the Universal Mind – Akashic Records. We merely need to utilize it.

Another level of psychic communication is a "feeling," such as when you walk down the street and you know that if you turned around there would be someone looking at you. Understanding this feeling as correct may be of enormous help. It may even turn out to be a friend that you would have otherwise missed seeing. The principle of the psychic communication at work is to listen to the input and then utilize it.

There is a "knowing," as displayed when you have an urge to stop in a store and then by "accident" run into a business contact, when previously you could not even get the person on the phone.

There are many contributing factors to what psychic communication means on a personal level. You need to trust your feelings and then to act on them.

Maria D'Andrea's Secret Occult Gallery
And Spell Casting Formulary

Man's culture has produced numerous responses on the psychic level. For example, when working with Spirit, herbs, gemstones, etc. was accepted, there were more people working with the concept. If in our society it is considered "normal" and accepted, then we feel comfortable developing psychic ability. However, if you lived in Salem at the wrong time in history, then obviously this was not the time to tell others you "know" things they do not.

Animals have always sensed danger and ran before actually seeing the enemy. We must have had the same ability on a higher level during times when it was much more needed. There must have been some level of this for cavemen to survive all those dangers besides just intellect.

Psychic communication has always been with us. It is merely a matter of your outlook.

So do pay more attention to your feelings. Utilize them. Then your life will go much more smoothly and happily. Trust in yourself and in where the information is from: Divine Power.

Maria D'Andrea's Secret Occult Gallery And Spell Casting Formulary

Guided By The Spiritual Realm

Spiritual Guides come in many forms and guises. They come as protectors, for spiritual guidance or to give us information. Spiritual guides are positive entities and may be someone who knew us and cared about us but have now passed on. The entity may be someone of another place or time or one who has never incarnated. There are also angels to watch over us at different times when needed or when you call on them.

Through the help of my guides, I am a trance medium and do automatic writing among other things. I have found that my spiritual guides are always there to help when I do anything on a psychic level. They are also there at numerous other times in my life. Knowing that both my sons, Rick and Rob, are watched over also makes my life as a parent less hectic and easier. As they are developing their own psychic powers, they will know that wherever they are, they are never alone.

When you feel that you have a guide, concentrate on the thought that you will allow positive entities only to be near you, as long as it does not hurt you mind, body or soul. Affirm that if the entity is negative or harmful, you order it to go away now. You have the decision. In this way, you will protect yourself from being influenced by anyone when you may not be sure of the intentions.

There are also diverse ways of communication. Some people "see the spiritual guide" and "know" what information they are supplying. Others are clairaudient and yet others go into a trance state. In a trance, you are not aware of the information. With your permission, the guide is able to give information to others through you as a channel.

Automatic writing is yet another way of communication. In this instance,

Maria D'Andrea's Secret Occult Gallery
And Spell Casting Formulary

the person allows the guide the use of his hand. He does not lose awareness and the pen (or typewriter) moves without the person being consciously aware of what the next sentence or perhaps word or letter will be. It is as much new information to the person as it is to others that read the material.

There are several reasons for having a spirit guide or guides. One reason may be due to the person being on a higher consciousness level, or in the process of developing psychically. If you are developing along this line, you may find that through automatic writing or other means you are able to give accurate, insightful information to help others.

Another reason is that you may be going through a stressful period in your life. This would be someone trying to warn and protect you. In this instance, the spiritual guide may only be with you for a short period of time. Some are with you for your lifespan or until you decide you do not feel comfortable and want the entity to go away.

They are not here to solve dilemmas. You need to make your own mistakes, to learn from them and to grow. The Karmic outlook is the belief that whatever you do, good or bad, will come back to you. We have free will so that we may learn to make the right choices and evolve spiritually.

Spiritual guides are attracted by us. Unlike with most people, assume it has to work both ways when you acquire a spiritual guide. You will usually attract a guide that is harmonious with you. However, let us say that you have attracted a guide that is negative. Then you will have to concentrate on only positive entities being around you, as I have mentioned before. The entity will have to leave. On the other hand, let us say that you are a person who does not believe that it is wrong to steal but the entity does. Once the entity is aware of the differences, it will simply leave. It has to be a situation where both feel comfortable with each other.

At times, you may get indirect information, an intuitive feeling or hunch. As an example, you may be on your way home and all of a sudden have a strong feeling or urge to stop and visit someone you may not even have thought of in a long time. If you give into this urge, you may find this person needed to talk to you about something important, or found something you left there and wanted to give it back to you. It may have been your spiritual guide prompting you to go for whatever reason.

Maria D'Andrea's Secret Occult Gallery And Spell Casting Formulary

A spiritual guide has access to information that many of us do not possess. They are able to tune into the Universal Mind, to see the past, present and the future. With some people there might be times, though, when they may get inaccurate information. As an example, if you are a trance medium, someone may ask your guide a question and get the wrong answer. Now, this does not mean that you are not a good medium. It only means that your spiritual guide is not infallible. After all, we are talking about spiritual guides who may not know everything, not about GOD.

When you do have a guide, it does not necessarily mean that you are being watched constantly. It is more when there is information to be passed on or you need to be guided or watched over. Also when you call.

We are not always the only ones aware of our guides. There are times when others who may be psychic will see them or feel their presence. Or just "know." At times like these, if you are not sure what your guide looks like or where the entity is from, ask the person for all the details they are able to pass on to you. You have to keep in mind also that they do not have our sense of time, so if you feel comfortable and it is also positive for the entity, the same one may be with you throughout your life.

Everyone has a spiritual guide to help when needed, when you need someone to guide you or to help you over some rough spots in your life; to help, not direct or make your decisions for you.

As the Bible says, in Psalm 91:11: "God will put his angels in charge of you to protect you wherever you go."

Learn to feel comfortable with your Guide and when you are not sure which way to go, know that there is someone there caring and guarding over you. Whether we understand it or not, through Divine Power everything has a place and a reason.

**Maria D'Andrea's Secret Occult Gallery
And Spell Casting Formulary**

The Secret Power Within Crystals And Candles

Two of the ancient sources of power and energy have been used in conjunction by metaphysicians in the secrecy of their sects. The use of both crystals and candles has been passed down as an Art. When these two are combined, the result is virtually unbeatable.

How often have you heard of Candle Magick, or of the force and energy of the crystals?

There is very real Power here to be utilized. The energy force of both is extremely strong. Think of it as being similar to electricity. Neither of them is seen by the naked eye. However, if you touch a socket you will feel the force of the electric current. If you send energy to help someone, the person will do well. Both are very real and physical.

Think of the candle as a Guiding Light and the crystal as the Power and Force to give it direction and focus.

Three extremely successful methods are as follows:

1. One way to use this knowledge is in meditation. As you meditate, keep a white candle lit in the room. This ascertains that only positive Spirit or information can come to you. It is a way of protection from anything negative. Also keep a quartz crystal within 3 feet of you. They attract or repel what you are working on. Out of this range, they work for whoever is closer. Just as a magnet, they do not discriminate. The crystal gives off an energy vibration to cleanse your meditation area. It will put you in touch with a higher level of consciousness.

2. The clear quartz is used for crystal gazing. It gives you a very strong, positive focus. The quartz crystal is said to have been used by Mer-

lin as a source of knowledge and control. When the quartz crystal is used simultaneously with a white and purple candle, it gives Power. The crystal ball or clear quartz crystal is placed in the middle, centered about 7 inches from both candles. The white candle purifies the energies and keeps things on a positive level. The purple candle brings in Higher Spirits and higher information. Mystics combine the forces and consciously work on the higher levels of the astral plane.

3. As a mystic, I find that, through a combination of methods, there is a vital need to have high energy. After all, if you are ill or lack the energy force on the level you require, then how can you control Power? Use this method to pull in energy when needed. Hold a clear quartz crystal in your receptive hand. Not the hand you write with. Close your eyes and visualize rays of white Light gathering in the crystal until you can feel it pulsating. Then visualize this White Light traveling up your arm and spreading throughout your body. As the energy travels, you will feel revitalized and full of energy and strength. At the same time, keep an orange candle lit near you. The orange color is associated with physical health and vitality. It is also the Life force being attracted to you. In yoga it is called Prana. The fallout effect of the color is that it also attracts prosperity.

Even if you are not working on a metaphysical level, there are always times in which you can use extra energy.

There is a variety of ways the candles have been utilized, among which are ceremonial magick, ancient religions, as well as in the Christian religion. This knowledge has been passed down through time.

The crystals have been in use as well in mojo bags, medicine bags, divination, protection, healing and as an energy source. Both are used by mystics and occult practitioners, anyone working with a Higher Source.

Try working with them and remember to only use the Power on a positive level.

Maria D'Andrea's Secret Occult Gallery And Spell Casting Formulary

Journey To Another Plane

Astral projection has always been somewhat of a mystery. People tend to either be in awe of the concept, or they reject it in its entirety, mainly due to the fact that it is not understood too clearly.

The fact is that you probably have to experience it yourself to fully comprehend. You really have to be aware that you have two bodies; an ethereal (astral) body and a physical one. The astral body has been said to be the true self with the physical shell as its home for now. The two bodies are united by a thin silver cord that is endless. In death, the cord is no longer united, thus setting the astral body free to go back to the spiritual realm.

Astral projection may or may not be a conscious effort. When there is a sudden death, the person may not have realized that they are no longer in a physical body. Also, during a trauma, such as an operation, there are persons reported to have seen their physical bodies as they hovered above.

When a conscious effort is made, you have to be very careful. Although you do not have to worry about the silver cord being severed and thus passing on, it does have its dangers.

First you have to either sit or lay down. Be comfortable and have your spine and head in a straight line. Then progressively relax. From your toes to the top of your head, make a conscious effort to feel your toes relax, your ankles and so on. You then need to have a clear destination of where you would like to be. Distance does not matter on this level. Breathe slowly and visualize your body being lighter, lifted up. Concentrate.

Your first sensation will be one of being pulled. Go with it. Some will feel a slow rising; some suddenly will see the ceiling closer. Others will get different sensations. Still others will get to their destinations immediately.

Maria D'Andrea's Secret Occult Gallery And Spell Casting Formulary

Most will get through slower and pass different planes. You will always feel that pulling sensation to get to where you wanted. Along the way there will be times when you will see things such as spirits. Do NOT stop to get a better look. It can be very dangerous. You can lose track of where you wanted to go and then get scared. This is the plane where clairvoyants and occultists work. There are forces that need to be understood. To be dealt with. It is a time to concentrate on your original destination.

If by chance you get scared or decide you want to go back, you automatically will. It is like being a rubber band. You want to be back and it snaps you back right away.

The astral plane is just as real to you as the physical to your physical body.

This is also where the Akashic records are to be found that store the knowledge of the past, present and the future.

Astral projection can be controlled and, when properly used, be of benefit and interest. Remember that you cannot stop off in your travels to look around. Just bear in mind where you want to go and you will find it a positive experience.

It has been known through the ages and used with varying degrees of control by psychics, occultists, magi and people from all walks of life. Astral projection is still in the midst of controversy and I suggest to anyone with an interest to stop at the library or their bookstore and open their awareness to a new dimension that is very much there.

Maria D'Andrea's Secret Occult Gallery And Spell Casting Formulary

Maria D'Andrea's Secret Occult Gallery And Spell Casting Formulary

Spell 3

Weakens Negative People And Keeps Negativity Out

This weakens and keeps people from getting to you in a negative manner. Also protects your home from intense negative energy.

Mix: Red Pepper

Cayenne Pepper

Sea Salt

Sprinkle the mix around the house. Keeps negativity out. Also put out as an affirmation and intent so that when you go in or through the house, this makes you and the ones close to you clearer and stronger.

Earth Changes And How They Affect You

Have you ever noticed that there are times when you are very moody? Some moments you simply do not feel like yourself? Perhaps you felt there is something wrong with you since there really was no valid reason for this feeling.

Be assured, it is NOT you. There have been persons going through these changes for centuries, wondering what is happening within themselves or just not being aware of the changes and only those around them wondering, "What happened to him?"

It is actually due to the changes in the earth. After all, we are also part of nature. We feel the pull of the tide and the effects of the full moon. This has been proven scientifically.

What we need to be more aware of is that the seasons also have their effect.

Have you given attention to the fact that during the winter you seem more emotionally indolent, compared to the summer? You feel like not getting up as easily in the morning, nor as fast. You may not want to do as much at an earlier time at night, due to the darkness being at a different time from the summer. Also, some have felt depressed or worried more easily. At this time, if you are going through these changes emotionally, it will be harder to pull out of them.

Whereas, in the summer, when we have all the sunlight and brightness, it will be more difficult to get upset, hurt or angry. Of course, if you do get agitated, it will pass faster. It is effortless at this time to see the "bright" side of things. When the change comes in the spring, there is more of an inclination towards romance, the urge towards children, towards the need

Maria D'Andrea's Secret Occult Gallery
And Spell Casting Formulary

to have a child. You will have a feeling of being unsettled. You will need changes at this time.

This is also a very good time to start a new business. The tendency for the business that is started now is for it to go very well. It may take a while but it will still have a progressive upward move.

You are also more aware of those around you than you were during the other months. You have a need to break loose just as the earth needs to. You will see flowers "breaking loose" from the ground, reaching towards a new beginning, just as we all are.

The fall finds us toning down. Emotionally, we get more careful, more protective of ourselves. We start at this season to look more inward. Actually, what we are doing is getting ready for the winter. This season will feel like a slowing down process. We will take time to look at the leaves changing colors, take time to look around us. <u>Take the time</u> to slow down a little more in our lives.

You will also notice that there is a season in which you feel more comfortable, a season that makes you feel better. That feels more the way you feel – that is you. That will be a good season for you to start any new projects, new romances.

We need to look at nature and to see and feel what is going on each year. When we are aware, then we can learn to have more control over our own lives.

Maria D'Andrea's Secret Occult Gallery And Spell Casting Formulary

Stones Of Intrigue

Stones and their influences have been with us since ancient times, when they were an exact science. The vibrations were utilized for varied reasons; spiritual, mental and physical.

The same stone may have varied effects on different people, depending on the person's vibration. It should also be noted that to see the results will take time.

We are coming full circle and rediscovering the ancient sciences, the lost arts. Actually, we never really lost them. Much of the information was not widely known, but only by a select few. Also, due to the political atmosphere, depending on the time in which you are looking, the information simply went underground.

With the use of the stones you can attract anything into your life.

The vibrations of some gemstones are known for their aid in meditation, some for their healing powers, others for protection, higher consciousness, love, money, luck and many diverse reasons.

The stones have been in use for numerous reasons all this time. First, because they do work, then also for their durability, color and financial worth.

Stones have physical vibrations. Due to this they attract other vibrations that are in their vicinity. Thus they heighten our sensitivity. Or they can send out their vibrations and thus influence our physical bodies or environment.

For the stones to work for you they need to be worn or within three feet of you. You can carry them with you in your pocket, pocketbook, the small bags used in occult work, etc. You may wear them as jewelry, amulets,

Maria D'Andrea's Secret Occult Gallery And Spell Casting Formulary

or talismans as long as they are within three feet, the range their vibration needs. Otherwise, they will attract what you need to the person who happens to be closer to them.

When you want or need certain things in your life you can simply look up which are the most appropriate and utilize them.

Whatever you can conceive you can find a stone for. As an example:

    Sodalite: Luck, peace, harmony

    Quartz Crystal: Protection, love

    Snow Quartz: Purity, helps to break bad influences (smoking, drinking...)

    Tiger Eye: Good luck, protection

There are numerous others and more than one use for many of them.

There is a mineral called staurolite. This was also called Baseler Taufstein or baptismal stone, known for its use as an amulet at baptism. It is also called Fairy Cross. They have been worn as charms and they look like a cross. They are formed in that shape by nature and when mined, they already look like a cross. There are many stories associated with this stone, stories of fairies playing by the spring when a messenger elf came and told them about the crucifixion of Christ. They were all so sad that they cried. Then their tears turned into the form of a cross. There are many such stories.

Experiment. See and feel the effect of a stone vibration on you and know that as they bring in what you want, you can also have fun with them.

Maria D'Andrea's Secret Occult Gallery And Spell Casting Formulary

Alpha Reality

There are levels of awareness that we can consciously put to use. Beta, which is our normal, everyday brain wave level. Alpha and Theta, which is where psychic occurrences happen, and Delta.

These are altered states of awareness. It is as though you were seeing two realities, both equally real. One is the material reality and the other is Alpha reality. It is merely an ability to tune in.

The average person only uses ten percent of his potentials. With your brain wave on Alpha, you can use more and brighten and heighten this level and are able to put it to positive use to help yourself and others.

First you need to learn how to relax your body and mind to block out sensory impulses, to develop your subconscious, and so to develop super-awareness.

You need to block out your mental thought process. You cannot do two things at the same time. If you are thinking you cannot go down to deeper levels within yourself just as you cannot do so if your legs are cramped since your thoughts will then be centered in that direction.

One of the most effective ways to tune into Alpha is to meditate. First visualize and feel yourself inside each color of the rainbow (red, orange, yellow, green, blue, violet). With each color go deeper into yourself. Then slowly count backwards from 20 to 1. Feeling more and more relaxed and going deeper. When you get to one, visualize a door in front of you. Go through it and into a comfortable room with a big white screen.

Here is where you will see your past, present and future. If you need to solve a problem, as an example, you would put the problem on your screen

Maria D'Andrea's Secret Occult Gallery
And Spell Casting Formulary

and give it a little time to give you a way to solve it. The answer will come to you.

There is the Infinity of the Universe in all of us and so we are all connected, tuned in. When you go down into your levels, you acquire the ability to create, heal, and understand. If you want to reorganize your negative habits, you visualize it in a positive way on the screen, and your subconscious sees both as reality (Beta and Alpha). It also takes everything literally. Through visualization and meditation it will accept your input and change your life outwardly. Your body and consciousness will respond quickly.

We are responsible for our thoughts, which cause these changes. Remember, "Ask and ye shall receive, seek and ye shall find, knock and the door shall be opened." This is a very real way of working with your life.

Alpha solves problems after your consciousness says, "I give up! Help!" It balances you physically, mentally and emotionally.

It is a positive way to acquire what you want or need and to help others.

As Emerson said, "Be careful of what you wish for or you may get it." With practice you will go into Alpha faster. Work with it and be constructive.

Maria D'Andrea's Secret Occult Gallery And Spell Casting Formulary

UFO's And Crystals

Most people are not aware of the strong connection between crystals and UFOs, although the ties have been there through the ages.

According to some legends, the quartz crystals were considered magickal stones. They were used for precognitive dreams, clairvoyance and numerous other forms of divination. Among occultists and mystics these stones are called "the philosopher's stone."

The quartz crystal has varied uses, such as:

1. Breaking up white light
2. Healing
3. Utilized as a memory bank
4. To disrupt a laser beam
5. Used for high energy
6. Application with electricity – to break or strengthen
7. Utilized for telepathic messages
8. As a crystal ball
9. On the end of a power rod to send energy and control nature elements
10. For protection
11. Attraction of what you want in your life

The quartz crystals have a natural ability to disrupt, amplify and blend energies.

Among these energies are magnetic and electrical fields.

Scientists are now "discovering" the power and distance these crystals can work with. Technically, the scientists look at this as a result of the crystals' piezoelectric property. It is said that this property enables us to blend our consciousness with the energy forces of the universe on an electromagnetic level.

If we can control the energy, it stands to reason that there must be other beings, extraterrestrials, that may also have recognized this ability.

Some theories conclude that there were ancient people on our earth who were not originally from this planet. They came from a faraway planet much like our own. The main purpose of their visit here was to study and to gain knowledge of this planet and the life it supports, much as our scientists have done in a much limited way in exploring other planets.

So their starships, UFOs, landed and colonized this green planet. With them they brought their culture, their science and their way of looking at life, their perspective being understandably varied in many ways from our own. It would have to be if you consider all the knowledge it would take to be able to get here.

Just think, these extraterrestrials came, perhaps light years from their homes, to discover and to learn (a very human quality). They came with peace in their hearts, surrounded by knowledge and in the White Light.

How else could they be so peaceful?

Let us look back at those times in ancient days. If these extraterrestrials intended to be aggressive or a dominant race, they most certainly could have accomplished that outcome with ease. To travel through space to an underdeveloped world, with as yet simpler humans, and not take charge, they would have to be advanced in spirit.

Ancient beliefs seem to support the stories of extraterrestrials. Look at some of the myths pertaining to Gods and demigods, heroes. They all express the benevolence of these people and their love. They surely must have looked at us as children.

Maria D'Andrea's Secret Occult Gallery And Spell Casting Formulary

While on their expedition, they needed to make contact with their own people.

Archeologists have uncovered many artifacts. Nothing that they would consider as operated for use by the UFOs for communications transmissions, but then what are they looking for? Something that they feel is very scientific looking and advanced? Maybe with metals we do not have on this planet?

Realistically, we know planets are from the same basic structure. Also, they simply could be looking directly at the source of transmission and not realize what they are looking at.

It would seem that, concerning these colonies, some either chose to stay or they were simply stranded. However, they could still communicate with their home planet.

To mankind at an earlier time, seeing the communication process and not understanding what they were witnessing, it must have looked like a ritual to be copied, held in reverence and passed down.

One of the methods we are aware of is to utilize the quartz crystal. This was done by wearing a certain type of headband. Probably the wearer would look towards the stars as anyone communicating looks toward home. There are still high priestesses who go to the mountaintops (higher elevation towards home perhaps), lift their outstretched arms toward the sky and communicate with an unknown source wearing something around their foreheads.

This communication device is one containing a quartz crystal. You may construct this in the ancient way or modernize it.

To make it as was the custom you need the following materials:

1. A clear terminated quartz crystal on one end only.

2. A flat piece of copper about half an inch wide and long enough to fit around your head at least of the way around

3. Two small pieces of leather

4. Round flat piece of copper, approximately the size of a quarter

Take the terminated quartz crystal and place it in a glass or bowl with

Maria D'Andrea's Secret Occult Gallery And Spell Casting Formulary

about 8 ounces of water. It should also contain seawater, and about half a teaspoon is enough. Then place this in direct sunlight for three consecutive days.

This process will cleanse the stone of any negative vibrations which may have been carried over from a previous owner, store or location. When this is done, proceed to the next step. You need to wrap part of the round copper piece around the bottom of the quartz crystal with the terminated part not covered and point up. Then either use a soldering iron or other method to melt the round copper piece into the center of the flat headband. You could also use some type of adhesive used with copper. You could also cut a big enough slit in the middle of the flat headband to insert the quartz crystal, termination point up, and press it around the stone to hold it in place.

Next, make a small hole at each flat end. In each hole insert a piece of leather. Now you can tie it to hold it in place when wearing it. A simpler method is to wear the terminated quartz crystal when it still points up to the sky, placed in the middle of your forehead where you have your third eye. Then hold it in place with either a scarf or a headband.

Next, sit or stand in a comfortable position. Relax. Put up psychic protection. Do not concentrate at first. Put the thought out that you want to communicate with whoever is out there, extraterrestrial. This could also be used for telepathy with someone you know if they also have a band to amplify the thoughts and vibrations.

Then repeat it a few times and wait, knowing it will come. Then feel as if you are waiting for a phone call. You will be surprised at the information you may receive through this method.

Perceive it as a device to help you tune in a higher level. It strengthens and amplifies your mental abilities and psychic talents.

The quartz crystal is clear or almost clear in color. It is found all over the world, including the United States. Chemically, it is also known as SiO_2. The stone has easy access as it also must have had so long ago.

Another method you could use is in a layout form. You will need:

1. A larger terminated clear quartz crystal

Maria D'Andrea's Secret Occult Gallery And Spell Casting Formulary

    2.   Two smaller terminated clear quartz crystals

    3.   One smoky quartz crystal. The shape does not matter. It can be a raw stone.

Proceed to cleanse the stones as previously directed for three days. Next, place them in a triangle formation, with the larger clear crystal forming the top point and the other two forming the two points at the base. Next place the smoky quartz crystal about halfway between the two smaller, clear crystals along the triangle base.

Relax. Do your protection. Place your hands on the outside of the triangle or on both sides, palms facing in towards the center. Look at the large, clear crystal and ask to be in touch with any positive beings. Repeat this on and off. Keep looking into the crystal and see what you feel, hear, sense or see. Information may come in varied forms. Be open to them and if you have a question, ask it. Wait a minute and repeat it. It may take a little while before you receive an answer. After all, if you ask your friend next door a question, your friend may also have to take a minute to think before answering you. Think of this along the same lines.

You are sending out a message or question. Have a little patience for the reply, although with a few people it may come fast.

Sometimes through the crystals they will send information which sounds like a sermon or something along those lines. This makes sense when you think of it. There is a Higher Being in our belief system. If there is more than one planet, more than one life form other than us, especially on a more progressed level, wouldn't they also know this?

If they are extraterrestrials on a higher Spiritual level, they would want to pass down this awareness to a planet still in a developmental phase.

They came as teachers previously. Some occult formulae have existed for centuries and must have been passed down from these beings.

For instance, they say there is a magick stone that Gods give us as a gift, a gift to remember we are connected by the White Light. When we are alone we need to take this magick stone and sit comfortably on the ground at noon. Hold the stone in the middle of your two hands placed next to each other. Hold your palms up. Look into the stone and think of the White Light

Maria D'Andrea's Secret Occult Gallery And Spell Casting Formulary

within us.

As you look you will see a glow within the stone. It is the confirmation that they can hear you. This stone is the clear quartz crystal.

They say the "Giant" people came to Atlantis from a distant star. They brought a stone with them which when held in various positions could send pictures at a distance (much like television), send sound waves to communicate (ancient radio). When aimed at individuals, it sends a healing ray. This was and is a many faceted giant crystal.

From this information of the past many valuable formulae are still stored and waiting to be put into use.

There is a harmony, a balance between the stars. All of nature has this balance. Certain notes and colors correlate to the planets. Numbers, vibrations and numerous other elements – one being the quartz crystal and the others being of different shapes, forms, colors and sizes.

The basic composition which the planets consist of are similar so we have the supposition that what one planet has, such as the quartz crystal, may also be feasible to be on another planet so it would also carry in thought over to extraterrestrial beings.

After all, if you can work with clay, then you can work with it wherever you are. The ability and knowledge goes with you always.

Another form of contact can be made through the smoky quartz crystal. Place a smoky quartz in your open hand. The shape of the quartz is unimportant as long as the surface is smooth on one side at least. Hold it so the smooth surface is facing up from your hand.

First, remember to always cleanse the stones you work with.

Place the stone in the hand you would normally write with.

If you use both, then decide which is a little stronger or used more often.

Close your eyes and feel the vibrations of the stone. Let the energies flow through you, surround you. Let them blend with your energy. Now concentrate on the information you want from your contact. Such as:

Maria D'Andrea's Secret Occult Gallery And Spell Casting Formulary

What is your name?

What do you look like?

Where is your planet located?

What does it look like?

What does your home look like?

Your age?

You can ask any number of questions but ask one at a time. First ask one, then repeat it a few times. Three times should be enough.

Still keeping your eyes closed, place the smoky quartz in your passive hand. This is your receptive hand. This is used for receiving, being open to information coming in. Your other, dominant hand is for sending energy and information.

Hold the stone in your receptive hand for a few minutes to get your answer. This will come in many forms, such as:

1. Seeing a scene unfold in your mind
2. Hearing information you previously did not know
3. Knowing a sense of inner trust

Really pay attention to the information. Write notes as soon as you are done otherwise you may remember some of the information but not all or not as clearly.

When you get an answer then go on to the next question. Remember, you will not always get an answer. After all, if you telephoned a friend, is that person always there to answer? If you ask a question, that person may need to go to the library to look it up or just will not answer because of lack of knowledge in that area.

Do not limit yourself to one area of questions, as there may not be answers forthcoming. However, if you ask questions about various subjects, there will be an interest shown.

Ask about the White Light, as an example. This seems to permeate through our information and the connection is there with the crystals.

Maria D'Andrea's Secret Occult Gallery And Spell Casting Formulary

Questions should be asked along the lines of:

1. When – Example: When did this take place?
2. Where – Where did it happen? Where is it?
3. Why – Why did this occur?
4. How – How was it handled? Solved? How does it look?
5. What – What was the cause? Outcome?

Also ask how you can be helpful. Is there any particular time to get back in touch in order to acquire the best results?

You will find that 11:00 a.m. and p.m. to 12:00 a.m. and p.m. as well as 4:30 a.m. or p.m. to 5:00 a.m. to p.m. to be more conducive. But experiment and find which is best for you.

Think of the crystals as battery chargers. You can make contact without the crystals if you are a psychic, as an example. Otherwise, it will bring you in tune and will amplify your thoughts, good or bad, to send information.

This can be sent as verbal, thought, or visualization. See which you feel more comfortable with, or with numerous methods. Do not limit yourself as to how you are getting the information. The point is to get it.

UFOs have been spotted for centuries. There are many hundreds of books and articles on them as they are researched. The various branches of the armed forces have them on record.

To help you make contact with them, keep a crystal in your house. It is like having a beacon or a homing device, whether on a communications level or as landing points.

The crystal sends out its own vibrational energies. It can be utilized as a focal point.

Before you sleep, do psychic self-defense then repeat to yourself a few times: "I am now put into touch with a positive extraterrestrial being. I am calm and relaxed."

Take 2 or 3 deep breaths then say, "I will remember everything clearly and precisely when I awaken."

Upon awaking put your information on paper. You may get information concerning your future or that of others. You may start "seeing" personality traits of the one you are dealing with, the same being, consecutively. Give yourself a focal point to start yourself off. You may also discover that at certain phases of the moon you are more receptive than at other times, or you are more easily able to "send," also, at certain times of the year. This could be due to varied distances from numerous stars at each time.

We are all star children working from different vehicles. The full potential has yet to be realized. Why not be the one to tap into it and make the discoveries which are long awaited?

Maria D'Andrea's Secret Occult Gallery And Spell Casting Formulary

Spell 4

Sea Magick For Any Wish

Use damp sand to form into shapes which represent your wishes. Focus on your wish while forming shapes.

Then let it be washed out to sea to carry that energy on every wave.

Also an effective process when you are working on wearing down an illness.

When it is dry, you can also hold it in your hand, focus on your needs and release it saying, "I send this desire to the wind and water to transport my desire."

**Maria D'Andrea's Secret Occult Gallery
And Spell Casting Formulary**

Colored Lights - How Your Exposure To Them Can Affect You

Have you ever considered why you have more energy at times or mood swings? Colors affect us more than we sometimes give them credit for.

When you are at a party, your mood can be different if they have a red light bulb or even a red rug. A red rug in a room always makes you feel like staying longer. The red bulb will intensify your mood. If you are emotionally down, you will be more so. If you have a high level of energy, it will become higher.

Knowing the varied effects of colored lights can be very beneficial. You can put the knowledge to conscious use.

I find colored light blue bulbs are a simple way. For a full force effect, you would sit under or close to the colored bulb. Never for more than 15 to 20 minutes at one time. You do not want to overbalance your system. However, you can do so more than once a day.

Sit under a green light, the color of grass green. If you do so, it will speed your natural healing process. It will not cure you, but it will speed things up. As an example, if you have an injured arm and it will heal in eight weeks, then use the green. Now, it will heal in approximately four to five weeks. You would use the light at least once a day.

For increased energy, you would use an orange light. The orange shade is the spectrum. Your energy will be higher. Sometimes when you have many things that need to get done your energy may not be there. However, you would not use it constantly, since it will be the same as working against your natural physical system.

Maria D'Andrea's Secret Occult Gallery
And Spell Casting Formulary

To increase your ability to study, you would use yellow, the shade of the sun. This will help you increase your level of learning faster and retaining the knowledge longer compared to your normal level.

Blue light, the shade of the sky, will bring inner peace and calm. It will also aid you in increasing your ability to communicate, such as when you need to give a lecture, or make an important point to your boss or friend.

Red light also increases your physical strength and sensuality. You do not want to spend more than the time span recommended since it will over-balance due to it being able to over-stimulate. This is a color to use with caution. You should follow it with a calming color such as blue. Blue will also heighten your level of intuition. It is good for lowering your heartbeat rate and to counter colds. It is the color of the bridge between two worlds: this reality and the metaphysical (spiritual) reality, both equally real.

Everything has a vibrational frequency. You will notice yourself how seasons have their own colors. Now being in a room with certain colors can shift your mood.

Apply this so you can be one step ahead. Why be in a bad mood when you can use the vibrational influence of the yellow light and be more cheerful?

Violet is a spiritual color. It will give meditation a stronger or deeper level. It also helps to control excess hunger. St. Germaine was said to help mainly with this color. It stimulates psychic ability.

Try the colored Lights yourself to get their feel. Be more aware of your color surrounding and be conscious of how their vibration influences you.

You can avoid an argument knowing the red Light is interchanging with your vibration of already being in a mood to be by yourself.

So set the moods consciously and also have some yellow Light at a party to insure a happier group of people. Have fun with it!

Maria D'Andrea's Secret Occult Gallery And Spell Casting Formulary

Wind Magick

There have always been people who had the ability to control and work with nature.

We are able to do so through an understanding of the Cosmic Law, an awareness of how to control your own energies first, then how to put them to practical use.

We blend with nature and direct it. It cannot be forced.

In Europe there is a belief that you can stop the wind by tying its energy up with a rope. Certain knots give you control, such as to calm ships at sea, for a positive control and purpose.

In Greece they tie the wind in a wind bag to be used as needed.

American Indians move the air in energy waves with their hands. They believe it gives protection and spiritual information. Some tribes such as the Navajo believe in the Wind People, spirits who deal with holy people to guide and give information.

These beliefs, as well as those of other cultures, use sympathetic magick, which involves going through the outward motions to express what the needed outcome will be.

There is an affinity in nature's Law between everything, the universal forces being all connected.

Men and women with the ability to use will power have the control over nature and thus can manifest their needs.

Today in our society there are those of us who still utilize this ancient knowledge, including some who aid others without their awareness of a cata-

Maria D'Andrea's Secret Occult Gallery
And Spell Casting Formulary

lyst being in control.

The ability is to be taken seriously. It is not meant to be played with or for show.

It is to be utilized for positive purposes, such as to invoke the spirits for information and aid.

There may be a decision that you cannot make and it affects others. Calling in the spirit guides to give you directions on the best move for the benefit of everyone is a positive move.

You may need insight into your own life as to what should be the next steps to take.

Some magi work with ceremonies and rituals, others by their own methods.

Wind magick is in practice today and will be with us in the future, sometimes with society being aware, sometimes underground. As long as there are those who pass the knowledge on and those who psychically tune into The Source for information, the ability will never be lost.

We should all learn to work with nature to benefit ourselves and our planet. At least, we should look around and be aware of all that nature offers us and utilize it on a positive level. Use only what you need to since we are guests passing through.

Maria D'Andrea's Secret Occult Gallery And Spell Casting Formulary

Choices On Your Path

Love is the strongest universal force. It is your highest form of Power. We make the choice every day in varied situations regarding whether we will use this power.

Our lives are made up of conscious and subconscious decisions. As men and women, we have the God-given power of free will; not only do we make choices that affect the NOW but also our present and future Karma. We are not left to flounder on our own. We can receive help anytime we choose to have it. Even when we are not seeking it, we receive input.

Have you ever noticed your first gut feeling or instinct is always correct? It is showing you the best path for you. However, it is your own free will that decides to move on this or not. The information is a guide.

Make your choices consciously to listen to the indwelling Lord, to better your life on all levels, spiritual, material, emotional, physical and mental. When you call His name, He is always there. To help, protect and guide. It is still your own choice to move on your awareness or not.

We all need to progress at our own speed, on our own levels and paths. However, we can heighten these faster by listening to the Master Creator.

Looking back in our lives, we as children listen to our earthly father, knowing he will help when possible. How much more so then will our Divine Father help us? When there is an important crossroad in your life, be at peace. Meditate and try to let yourself relax then think of all the various aspects and call His name. Seek the guidance of the indwelling God. You will receive an answer either then or at a later time, but the answer will come. Sometimes you do not connect the answer when it comes to your seeking. As an example, you may have an urge to contact someone to use a certain approach in negotiating a contract that you "feel" is right. At other times you may receive sudden insight or simply "know."

Someone may come into your life at the right time to help, give helpful advice or perhaps bring in the right contacts. When you ask, keep your awareness open to the answer then move on it. Once it comes in you need to take action for the outcome to be the best.

The aid in making choices is our strongest defense to improve our lives in every way and protect us from negative people and influences. With all the people we have around us, it is still strictly our own choices that influence how we move on our Path of Life. Learn to trust the "I AM" presence and watch your life start to move upward. You can actually keep track.

Maria D'Andrea's Secret Occult Gallery And Spell Casting Formulary

The Call To Ministry

Most are unaware of the strong urge that pulls us to become ministers.

Many of us work from a psychic or intuitive level, as did the ministers in the beginning. The apostles did not work strictly from an analytical point of view. I find that I was aware of the legalities of becoming ordained years prior to having the urge to do so. I became ordained when the time was "right" for me. It was the call to service. I find that I look at it as being a minister of the Light, the Godhead being the source. Even if we can show the way to just one person to be positive and understand the Path of Light, we have already accomplished much. I feel in this way we are lighting up the world one Light at a time....

"The Lord is God, and He has given us light." Psalms 118:27.

As counselors we help those who come to us on a religious, psychological and intuitive or psychic level. Not only do we work from intellect, but from empathy, understanding and Divine Guidance. We tune into the source within us and "Let go and Let God" handle the situation. We are not alone and need not approach problems by ourselves. We may have problems that are financial, emotional, health-related, that involve some kind of injustice or of any other need. We listen to the voice within to guide us. God is always there to help. As is written in Psalms 55:22: "Cast your burden on the Lord, and He will sustain you."

As a minister, I always work with a continuous Prayer List. You need to feel what is correct for you, but when you have the power of prayer, you are working with force. You simply have people with a request or need write them out for you with their names, then you pray for them each day with sincere intention. You do need them to send a donation, to keep the energy flow. I do so for one month.

As a professional psychic, I also conduct Prayer Circles. At that time, I add the names of the people on the Prayer List. You cannot over-do prayers. You are always heard.

When you feel the need to serve others, that urge to be ordained as His minister, remember that this is the main way to know you are ready. After all, the apostles did not go to school for years to become the ones who could preach the Word. It came from their hearts and the indwelling Lord.

Remember whether you are ordained or not to always stay on the positive Path and Listen to the Divine Guidance coming from within you.

Maria D'Andrea's Secret Occult Gallery And Spell Casting Formulary

UFO's On The Astral Plane

Most people consider UFOs as only physical. They need to see proof, but when it does come they do not acknowledge it.

On the physical level, we already have abundant proof for those who wish to see. There are cave drawings depicting people in what we know to look like space helmets. Stories, myths abound with visitors from the sky. The myths are similar throughout the world, with cultures too distant from each other to affect one another's stories.

There are also myths of Light Beings coming to impart aid and information, prophecy, healing and warning. In some cases these Light Beings are considered on such an everyday basis and for such a length of time that we realize the contact could not have been with just one person or a form of group hysteria.

In ancient times, people were closer to nature, more aware, as are the Native Americans and Metaphysicians that are part of the earth, not believing that we own or control it.

Being more in tune, dealing with Light Beings was not such a shock or as much outside of the normal outlook.

Physics and myths correlate on some of the same points. They describe these beings as formed of white light energy, as shimmering light bodies you can see through, of a feeling of love and protection and in some cases a paternal feeling emanating from them.

Communication worked on two levels – one on a verbal level as our normal method of communication and the other as telepathy. The information being passed on through clairaudience, or images which our minds immediately attach words to, is part of our cultural response.

There seems to be more than one area or level that they came from. Psychics have picked up emanations from the Light Beings from pieces of meteorites. In Egypt, they let the people know that they originated from a different galaxy, some in physical, others in Light form.

One of the ancient methods of communication passed to us from that time is still with us, known as a crystal headband used by priestesses of Egypt to heighten their telepathic ability to communicate beyond the stars for enlightenment, aid and information. We similarly need to send "sensitive" people to explore beyond the stars for enlightenment, aid and information. If you have an astronaut land on a planet and not see anything physical, he will say it is a dead planet, without life form. However, a sensitive person may see spirits or Light Beings and thus have a very different outlook. After all, even on our earth we have always had people who are able to see both realities, the physical plane and the astral plane. They can communicate with the non-physical energies.

There are varied energy levels on earth. In the universe the same cosmic laws would be at work. With the New Age, the Aquarian Age coming in, there will be more people becoming aware. Meditation is now an accepted form from occultists to businessmen. It helps to tune us into the higher sources, meditation being the bridge between the two worlds. Some believe angels are one of the Light Beings we communicate with.

When reading past stories, some mention them as taking on physical forms, coming down in a round cloud shape. When you look at details they are similar to UFO sightings.

We need to keep an open mind concerning both planes. Those who do not wish to see will not under any circumstances do so. However, those with an open mind will gather their own input and then decide on what their belief is.

There are too many fables, myths, stories, and legends which are passed down from generation to generation to be ignored. For all the countries and histories to have so much in common, there has to be contained in them a basis or starting point for the truth.

Maria D'Andrea's Secret Occult Gallery And Spell Casting Formulary

Maria D'Andrea's Secret Occult Gallery And Spell Casting Formulary

Spell 5

To Release Anger

Use lavender, chamomile or Lang Lang Oil.

Put a few drops on the bottom of your feet, because of the meridians found there.

On a white piece of paper, with black ink, write the words:

"Through Fire and the Power of the Sun, I now release all feelings of anger. I now replace it with harmony and balance. Releasing now clears my life to make way, as an open door, to all joy and happiness."

Do this on a Sunday.

Next, burn the paper to ashes (you may have to relight it a few times) and throw it to the wind to release anger so it does not harm you and depress you.

Maria D'Andrea's Secret Occult Gallery And Spell Casting Formulary

Forms With Power

Forms of power have always been with us. They are forms that are utilized as psychic tools due to their structure, such as a potential of their natural areas, the character of the shapes. They are formations of a unique way of power. Since before the ancients, they were used for information, guidance, counsel, power and protection when doing psychic work. They all have their own energy. Some of these forms are well known to all of us, such as the cross, circle, pyramid, cone and triangle.

One of the most well known and powerful stones of power are the ones forming the stone circle called Stonehenge. These are located in Salisbury, England, where once they were put to constant use. Stonehenge is a barren area on which are placed stone monuments in a circle. The placement was designed for observation of heavenly bodies and for predictions based on their movements, an astrological calendar, among other utilizations. Much as a pyramid, this structure measures the sun and moon positions in inner measurements to show exact solar years.

Stonehenge was believed to be a worship place for Kings and the Chiefs prior to them. Said to be connected to the Celtic culture and the Druids, these people, being extremely psychic, also worked with the heightened psychic levels of the monuments.

The stones themselves and their placements vibrating on a higher energy level would be a place to observe psychism in action where much of this activity is non-controlled.

Scientists, among others, are still working on finding out all the workings of these forms with power. One assumes the ancients were more versed in higher knowledge than most people in our time. Stones of all types have

Maria D'Andrea's Secret Occult Gallery And Spell Casting Formulary

the same elements as the human body and are thus compatible. We are aware that some stones, when placed near your body, will heighten your psychic ability, such as azurite. Others heighten different attributes. When you use words-of-power close to ordinary stones, even they will respond.

The cone-of-power is consciously worked with even in our time. This is a concentration of energy created by a circle of objects or of people. When the circle is continuous, it draws energy into the center. This can then be used for psychic purposes by sending it out through the conscious goals of the mind. This circle can also be drawn on the ground and worked with.

One of the forms of healing is a healing circle of people surrounding the ill person, thus sending a heightened energy level of healing.

The forms are too numerous to list and discuss although, with awareness of them, you do have a tool. Those of us who wish to use the forms of power need to consciously remember to use them positively and in a wise way. As they were used then, the forms of power are still utilized today. Use them to better your life and the lives of others.

Maria D'Andrea's Secret Occult Gallery And Spell Casting Formulary

Lucid Dreams

Lucid dreams have been with us since ancient times. Lucid dreaming is the experience of being conscious while being in a dream state.

Have you ever noticed that you can be aware that you are dreaming and still be in a dream state? This awareness is not very frequent among people. Some may never have a lucid dream, while others may have them two or three times a year. Others may have lucid dreams consistently. Lucid dreaming is accessible to people and can be a powerful tool and experience. We can open up, enjoy and utilize this ability.

There are varied approaches to dreams, some of which hold back our dealing consciously with dreams on a positive level. As an example, Freud and others had a standard approach towards dreams. They believed that dreams had a message from the unconscious. We need to analyze them and understand what they are telling us. This is also a positive way, since we can receive much input through dreams.

1. Psychic information: Can be precognitive dreams, telepathy

2. Physical: Most are about ourselves. We will get symbols that connect to how we perceive things. This can give information on solving ailments, such as soaking sugar cubes in fresh lemon juice to stop a cough.

3. Spiritual: Dreams which show us how to advance to a higher level. How to avoid a crisis.

4. Creative: As when a musician wakes up with the music he could not quite get correct, or seeing how to fix something in a better or newer way.

However, this limits us in some ways, since many feel that if we cannot analyze the dream, it is useless. So we look for people, books or tapes to explain the dreams.

The other limit we put upon ourselves is the supposition that we do not

Maria D'Andrea's Secret Occult Gallery And Spell Casting Formulary

have a choice in what occurs in our dreams, that we are not responsible for the dream. It happens to the dreamer. It is passive.

The formula for lucid dreams is entirely different. It is used frequently in dream therapy. You need to separate the dream into two parts rather than one. The one being <u>the dream</u> itself, while the other is <u>the dream and the content of the dream</u>

1. Content: Shows you how you can grow. To get better.
(not necessarily that we want to grow). Shows spiritual growth also.

2. Dreamer: Part of what is going on in the dream context. In lucid dreams you discover during your dreams that you are aware in the dream. You will wonder why you are more awake.

Think of these dreams as connecting the two realities or worlds. In this state you are standing on a margin between the two, such as people with near death or astral projection experiences. These people will experience seeing white light and will also experience a happy feeling.

Normally, in the dream state, if there is any discord, you will try to wake up. You may or may not succeed. If you feel you are about to die in a dream, you will automatically try to wake up since you feel you do not have any control within the dream. As you develop and are more aware, you will find you can continue through to an ending with your dream. You will know you cannot die and so you will have control. You can always wake yourself up if need be.

As an example, you are walking in the woods and enjoying the scenery. All of a sudden a fierce lion jumps out from between the bushes. It looks as though it will attack and kill you. Now you can deal with this in two ways. You can wake yourself up as you are accustomed to doing, or you can choose to go on until the end. When you continue consciously, decide how you want to deal with the situation. First visualize yourself as being calm and happy in the dream. Then decide what to do next. You can do a vast number of things, such as: letting the lion walk past you no longer being aware that you are there, or walking up to you and feeling that you are not a threat, letting you pet him. You have now changed the threat which was a symbol of some inner conflict. You come out victorious and now have the sense of that white light of peace and love, the white light being in all of us.

You went through a choice of proceeding with your dream on a positive level or running in fear. Look at what happened in your dream. How did you handle it?

Many people have a belief in the white light. In Yoga, the dream state is highly valued.

There is a point of leaving your body in dreams and heading toward the white light; a feeling of going home, of bliss, a feeling of awareness. It is reality and not an illusion.

To work with lucid dreams, you will go through varied levels:

1. Normal level: Not very active

2. Tension: When the dream has a little stress

3. Opposition: When you feel you will die in the dream. If you follow through instead then you will grow.

4. Yield: You can pray to have help to let everything go. It is the way to your deeper states of consciousness. You can experience Kundalini, the Oneness.

You need to be aware that you are <u>not</u> trying to change your dreams. They have a purpose. You are changing your reaction. You will become more positive in your attitude and outlook.

<u>How to achieve Lucid Dreaming – Always use psychic self-defense first.</u>

1. Meditate.

2. Make sure you get enough sleep.

3. Before you go to sleep, first state that you will have a lucid dream.

4. Choose a dream that reoccurs if you have had one and affirm that the next time it happens you will awake within the dream and be aware.

5. Experiment and have fun with it.

You will be on the path to Inner Growth.

Maria D'Andrea's Secret Occult Gallery And Spell Casting Formulary

Ghost Versus Spirit

Although most people are unaware, there is a difference between a ghost and a spirit.

Ghosts are earthbound spirits. They are people who have passed away. Some are aware of the transition and some still do not realize that they are not in their physical bodies. They are seeking help in crossing over to connect with the Godhead. There are those who are looking for a solution to a problem that existed in their previous life, unfinished business. Those who feel there are issues to be finished prior to their next step due to their passing on too soon.

Some are unaware they are in their Light bodies. Usually this occurs from a shock at the time of their demise, like getting run over by a car or any unexpected form. For instance, if they were ill for a long time then the subconscious would have expected it on some level instead of it being a shock. They need our help to become aware of their death.

This can be achieved simply by telling the ghost of its situation, then blessing this entity and sending it Love, Love being the strongest energy. Next, tell the entity to seek the White Light and head towards it. This White Light is the God presence. In essence, one is sending the entity home. You may need to repeat this process a few times for it to be accepted. However, the end result is always positive.

The word Spirit covers all levels, including ghosts. There are varied categories.

Elementals are one form. These are nature spirits, such as Devas, elves, nymphs, sylphs, undine, to name a few. These spirits connected to nature are very real. Their rate of vibration is very fast, thus they are difficult to test scientifically. The varied vibrational rates are acknowledged in the scientific field, this level being on the same wavelength as electricity. Some spirits have never incarnated unto the physical plane and some are entities who passed on from this life. Other spirits can attach themselves to negative people such as alcoholics, drug addicts, gamblers, etc. They can thus live vicariously through living beings.

Spirit guides come to those on a higher awareness level. They chose to serve, to guide us. They will give us information in varied forms such as clairvoyance, clairaudience, "knowing" or whatever form through which the person is open to receiving the information. The information is meant as a guide, not to tell us we "have to." They give us the knowledge but due to free will it is up to us whether we put it to use or not.

You may have noticed that around the time of Thanksgiving to a little after New Year's there seems to be more chaos on the spiritual plane. This is due to the spiritual world going through major changes. It is a time when higher spirit, Jesus, shows the way back to spirits through goodness, peace and Light. There is a balance in nature; yin and yang; positive and negative; light and dark; good and evil. Due to this it is a time of struggle for some in the spiritual world.

There is a hierarchy of angels and numerous other spiritual beings.

We need to remember that the ghosts are the earthbound spirits who need our help in first becoming aware of their own deaths, then in finding their way. If you are aware of this, then realize that you are in a positive position of aid instead of a negative situation when dealing with the ghosts.

Maria D'Andrea's Secret Occult Gallery And Spell Casting Formulary

Sounds Of Power

Various sounds have always been used in psychic and spiritual work. The utilization of these sounds is based on their ability to attract or repel whatever the situation calls for. There are various forms, all with positive results. Nature has a balance and so there are negative power sources as well, but we are not concerned with these at this time.

The use of drums is one of the oldest methods. Among others, magi, shamans, priests, spiritual workers all utilize this percussion instrument. It is used as an aid to invoke communication with the spirit world and to help a medium or sensitive to achieve a trance state. The drums have an effect on the nervous system due to the pulsating rhythm. They also repel negative entities as a form of protection due to their vibrational influences. This is called "sympathetic vibration."

Chants are another form. In Hinduism, the word "Aum" is one of power. It is the synonym for God. When chanted, it utilizes every part of the voice organs of every language. In essence, it represents the whole world. When chanting Aum (or Ohm, Om), we will vibrate through the Universe, thus helping you to reach numerous consciousness levels simultaneously. This Eastern chant is utilized by individuals, healers, and spiritualists for attunement. The vibrations charge the atmosphere with prana, which can then be directed for any specific purpose you choose.

American Indians use sound to correlate to nature. They utilize this power, as do Magi, Occultists, Mystics and Practitioners to control nature and to work with it.

Georgian chants were at their height in the Middle Ages. Originated by Pope Gregory for the Catholic Mass, each chant was geared to a specific religious purpose. This placed the congregation on an Alpha (psychic) level. Some of the chants placed people in an almost hypnotic state.

Maria D'Andrea's Secret Occult Gallery
And Spell Casting Formulary

We, as Mystics, use sound to invoke spirit, to manifest from thought (the Power of the Word, contained in the Bible) to physical (whatever we are working on at the time), to protect.

Music is another form. Notes are tuned into the planets, the universe, colors and various other levels. When a musician consciously creates for a metaphysical cause, the effect looked for will manifest. The intention may place you in a more meditative state prior to your meditation. It may place you in an Alpha state, to be more open psychically to information. Music also sets the mood. Have you noticed how certain songs make you feel mellower, happier, moody or "up"? Sounds have a very real effect on us and the universe.

Other words of power include; Ame, Amin, Abracadabra, Yahweh, Jesus, Nameste, Adonai, Tetragaematon, Bless You.

When you bless someone verbally you send positive energy; you seal the experience and it comes back to you on a blessing level. A blessing is psychic energy sent to a person or people for a constructive purpose, such as healing. It works on an electrical impulse on the one sent to you, transforming negative vibrations to neutral or positive ones.

The word Abracadabra in Hebrew represents the Father, Son and Holy Spirit. It is written in a triangle form (the Trinity). When used as an amulet around your neck, it protects and attracts good luck. The same word is used to heal and protect from physical illness in Aramaic.

This is one of the most frequently used words by occultists. It has the same vibrational power when written backwards.

Prayer is the strongest power source, whether it is The Lord's Prayer or one you made up. It is your direct link to Divine Power, to the Godhead.

Affirmations are also positive. An affirmation is a positive statement of prayer such as, God and I are One; I am one with all of life; the universe supports me; all my desires are met. Always remember that the vibration of sounds is to be utilized only as an aid, not to be confused with being the attainment you seek.

It is a tool to be put to use in conjunction with Spiritual Elevation. You may find sound to be of benefit to you. Try more than one form!

Maria D'Andrea's Secret Occult Gallery And Spell Casting Formulary

Symbolic Magick

Through the ages of occult work, imitation magick has been one of the most well-known and frequently used rituals, the theory being that by employing psychic abilities, one can influence the outcome of situations. "As above, so below." The symbol becomes what it represents.

Now this could be by visual effects, such as a picture of the person you are working on for increase in the person's financial condition. Also, the well-known doll to aid in healing.

Some farmers hang an ear of corn outside the edge of their fields to have the fields yield healthy and abundant crops. There can be other ways to represent your desire, where all of your senses can come into play, such as smell, color or any other sensation, whatever ways aid you to simulate an object, person, or event in a smaller version of your interpretation.

In nature, you will notice that one thing is affected by another, and when one aspect is not working in full force, it throws the balance off for everything else. It is all connected! As an example, if there isn't any rain in a farming area, the crops will not grow. There is lack of food for the farmer and he cannot sell the crops, affecting his financial situation and other people. They cannot buy his crops for food and he is unable to buy supplies from others, so he does not contribute to their income.

It is the same with magick. When you affect one aspect, you affect another by association.

The physical world is influenced by the non-physical. Think of it as a triangle.

1. We put the intention out by thought or the Word.

Maria D'Andrea's Secret Occult Gallery
And Spell Casting Formulary

2. It goes to the higher astral plane to manifest and form.

3. It comes back down to the material plane to hit, or to solidify as fact

There is no barrier of time or distance.

You can use an article of the person you work on to create a psychic link between

the item and the person. Then you can go through the activity you want to happen, using items such as hair, part of a shirt, picture, etc., and giving it the person's name. For healing, see the person well; first, put the person's broken leg in a small splint on the doll then visualize it getting better. Remove the splint and visualize the person well and happy through Divine Power. You don't actually heal the person; you speed up their natural healing process. Remember to use it ONLY for positive purposes. What you put out, you get back two-fold.

Try it to help others when you can, but only do so if it is meant from the heart and through Divine Power.

Remember we do nothing by ourselves.

Maria D'Andrea's Secret Occult Gallery
And Spell Casting Formulary

My Invisible Partner

Spirits have an energy body that is very real. The energy is tangible, just as we cannot see electricity but we know it is there as a physical force.

When it is possible, spirits will help us. I was working with detectives on a case that involved the murder of a man. His spirit helped to find the killers. His relative came to me to find out with the detectives how he died.

Holding a picture of him to receive psychic information, I looked up to "see" him standing in back of one detective. He showed visual aspects of the scene. He was in New York City, in a bar. He looked as though he was attempting to speak; however, I could not understand the words. He seemed to smile in understanding. Then I was looking at the scene as it actually unfolded. He was being attacked in the bar by two men and people were watching but not doing anything to help. There was a woman in the back of the room who felt connected with the men. During the fight, the man was killed and the two men and the woman ran out into the alley in the back of the bar. They were easy to describe now, having seen them. I also felt from the spirit that they were now in Kentucky in a blue van but not for much longer.

Upon checking, a few people in the bar that night admitted being a witness to the killing. The authorities in Kentucky were notified, just in case!

Due to the spirit's help, the three people were caught as they were about to leave the state. If it wasn't for the spirit trying to get through and sending a feeling of his presence and through his energy the picture of the crime, they would have gotten away, perhaps permanently.

When there is a Spirit trying to get through, you will sense it. Whether you wish to deal with it or not depends entirely on you. We have free will and this is a choice.

Maria D'Andrea's Secret Occult Gallery
And Spell Casting Formulary

At times it can be a difficult experience. We are all connected through energy. If you find you are dealing with a Spirit, ask it if it is positive. You will get an answer, a feeling. If you feel it is not, command it to go away NOW and it will. It is our choice. Remember, we are all made of energy in one form or another.

Maria D'Andrea's Secret Occult Gallery And Spell Casting Formulary

Spell 6

With An Angelic Spirit

First say a short Prayer For Protection. Say, "Divine Power Protect Me From All Harm And Negativity. Thank You."

Next, pick what area you are putting your intent/desire to, then choose one of the following Angelic Powers to work with.

For the purpose of:

Gaining more intellect, making better decisions, heightening your ability to speak in a professional or understandable way, ask Archangel Ariel to work with you and to bring in the Power of the Air energies.

For the purpose of:

Emotional balance, emotional situations, working with heart and chakra energies, ask Tharsis to work with you and to bring in the Power of the Water energies.

For the purpose of:

Dealing with properties, court cases, anything dealing with property, money, and farming, ask a positive Cherub to work with you and to bring in the Power of the Earth energies.

For the purpose of:

Heightening your energy, when tired and needing to heighten your ability to act, to take action for any reason, for romance, to heighten sexual levels, to increase ability to exercise better, ask a positive Seraph to work with you and to bring in the Power of the Fire energies.

Maria D'Andrea's Secret Occult Gallery And Spell Casting Formulary

Imagination Versus Psychic

Everyone has psychic ability. Some of us use it consciously while others may be unaware of its existence. The difference between the two is that imagination is mental first, whereas psychic ability is "seeing" first.

When you use your imagination, you visualize what you want in your life, what you want to happen that has happened, any number of unlimited things. You are aware that you plan what will be in your vision. When you daydream, you are using your imagination to visualize and decide mentally what you want next in your scenario. How you want to progress is strictly up to you. If you do not like the path you are taking, you simply change it to something else.

You can use your imagination in a positive way. This process is called "visualization." You can consciously imagine a situation you would like to be in, such as seeing yourself happy and glowing with health. If you would like to be in a positive relationship, see yourself with joy and with the type of person you would want to be with. Concentrate on this picture as many times a day as possible. This will give it force to be able to materialize. Make sure you only visualize positive things, so you do not build negative energy to come back full force to you. Also, be sure of what you want since you will get it.

On the other hand, when you are dealing with psychic pictures, the information is already there. You are very passive and do not have control over the input. It is much the same as a telephone when you are talking to someone. The person, the information it is for is at one end of the wire, and the information you receive is on the other end. You are merely the (channel) wire.

Maria D'Andrea's Secret Occult Gallery And Spell Casting Formulary

Have you ever noticed that your first hunch is always correct? That is psychic information. It is the same as someone telling you that the car you want to buy will break down. The information is there for you to use. Due to free will we need to decide which way to use the input. This gives you two options.

1. You can ignore the information and buy the car anyway. In which case, when something goes wrong, it was a conscious decision and you cannot blame anyone else for your problem.

2. You can use the information and either not buy that particular car or have it looked at and work something out such as lowering the price or getting the car fixed prior to the purchase. This is putting the psychic input to positive use.

Imagination and psychic ability can both be used in a positive way to improve our lives. Both are there as tools waiting to be put to use. Consciously work with both and keep track of the events as they unfold. You will be pleasantly surprised.

Maria D'Andrea's Secret Occult Gallery
And Spell Casting Formulary

The Friendly Visitor

I have found that when you are on a psychic level you are more open to "seeing" a ghost. Many times children will see them more often because they are not aware that they can NOT. As they get older it might lessen due to other people letting them know in one form or another that it should not happen.

When my older son, Rick, was about four years old he acquired a "friend." I would go past his room and hear one-sided conversations, or he would be in bed and might say goodnight to me and then to an unseen man. He could describe what this man looked like: tall, friendly, darker hair and so on. He would always describe this man the same way. At four years old, unless they actually see someone, children tend to forget some of what they said. They would just say whatever came to them at the time. Then he started talking to this man even if I was in the room, once in a while. First, my son asked questions. The first time he saw the man he was trying to go to sleep. He called me into the room to ask why the man was in his room. Then he wanted to know why I didn't see him. He really did not understand me. To him, this was as real as if one of his friends came over to play.

I asked him if he was scared, which he was not, and eventually he went to sleep. From then on, every now and then, the man would show up. Being on a psychic level helped considerably. I felt there must be a reason for this to happen since it did not seem to be a frightening experience. So I started to get into the habit of putting up a white shield, saying that I now put up a shield of God's white light of Love and Truth and nothing negative or harmful can get in, only positive and good. This way, if the entity was negative, it would not be able to come anymore; however, it persisted and my son did feel comfortable with this. I would find that when he "talked" to this man, if you were in the room, you could feel there was someone there with you.

At one time, when my son was older and in school, I realized this man did not come just when my son was there. I was walking through my living room and as I passed through the middle of the room, I walked around a man who was standing in my way and proceeded out of the room. As I entered the next room I suddenly realized that I just walked around someone who was not there. It was not an uncomfortable feeling but one more of surprise. It was also an intuitive feeling that it was the same man that my son was "seeing."

Rick is now 19 and we haven't heard from this man for a few years. He did come back on and off through the years so we really do not feel that we may never hear from him again. We just do not know. My son is a psychic, as is my eight year old, Rob. I feel that maybe this man is a help on that level since when a stressful situation comes up he tends to also come at that time. He also comes when there might be a psychic surge or phase that Rick is going through. Whatever the reason for him being here, I do get the feeling that it was his "choice" and he feels comfortable with it.

I find that there are many times that we really need to pay attention to what our children are saying, at all ages. It is also good to know that not all GHOSTS are negative or harmful. There are some spirits that are there to help or guide. Remember, there is a balance of negative and positive in all things, including the spiritual realm.

**Maria D'Andrea's Secret Occult Gallery
And Spell Casting Formulary**

Prosperity And Happiness Are All Yours
When You Are Guided By Spiritual Beings

Spiritual guides come in many forms and guises. They come as protectors (for spiritual guidance), or to give us needed information. Spiritual guides are positive entities, and could be someone who knew us and cared about us, but who has now passed on. Or, this entity may be totally of another place or time, one who has never incarnated. There are also the angels whose job it is to watch over us at different times in our lives, or when we call on them.

Through the help of my guides, I have become an accomplished trance medium who does automatic writing, among other things. I have found that my spiritual guides are always there to help when I do anything on a psychic level. They are also there at numerous other times in my life. Knowing that both my sons, Rob and Rick, are watched over makes life as a parent less hectic and easier. As they are developing their own psychic powers, they will know that wherever they are, they are never alone.

When you feel that you may have a guide, concentrate on the thought that you will allow positive entities only to be near you and this cannot harm your mind, body or soul in any way. Fully realize that if the entity is negative or harmful, you can order it to go way NOW, through Divine Power. The entity then must leave. It does.

**Maria D'Andrea's Secret Occult Gallery
And Spell Casting Formulary**

Healing: God's Natural Way To Perfect Harmony

The body heals itself. The body has the seeds within itself to respond to illness and heal itself. A healer can aid in speeding up this process.

All healing comes to us from Divine Power. We all have this ability within us. Some may use it subconsciously, such as those of us who rarely get sick, or when sick, have very fast recuperative powers. Others use it consciously on themselves or on others. The spiritual healer is one of these people and the healing comes in varied forms, depending on the method preferred by the healer.

Some use the laying-on of hands. Some work only on the aura around the physical body, while others heal at a distance. At times more than one method may be utilized.

The healing can only be done on those willing to be healed, otherwise you can send the healing energy but it will be blocked and not be put to use by the physical body. People, who are said to be medically incurable, have been cured or have found some relief from healers. Spiritual healers will be the first to point out that they are not the ones healing the person. The healer is much like a tool with the healing energy coming to the healer from Divine Power to flow through to the one who is sick. Some of the healers have spirit guides who come to aid and heal. That is not to say that the healing ability is not from God. The spirit guides who come are allowed by God to help. Usually their guides were doctors, shamans, surgeons, all healers of one sort or another.

The healer makes contact with the soul of the sick to make the person spiritually aware. If the person has a strong understanding of God, of truth, the healing will work. If there is much doubt or if the person within his or her heart does not really want the healing, the healing energy will not be allowed to work.

God gives all of us the option to be well and happy.

Absent healing can be done due to the energy to heal coming from the Godhead. Energy does not have a space or distance limit, much like electricity. It does not always need the wires, physical to physical, to touch and enable it to work. The ability to heal is there to be used either way, whether in the ill person's presence or in absence.

If your spirit is touched by the healing, you need to thank God from your heart for this manifestation. You can be healed even if it does not heighten your spiritual awareness, although this means that the person who had the illness missed a great opportunity to move upwards on the Spiritual path.

Healing can be done upon the physically ill, the emotionally hurt or drained, and the mentally tired or with problems. All cannot be healed, however, as we are all walking on our own Karmic Paths. However, if we acknowledge the Divine Power within us all, ask for guidance and help, we will receive it!

"For everyone who asks will receive, and anyone who seeks will find, and the door will be opened to him who knocks." Matt. 7:8

Healing is dominant throughout the Bible, as well as in every religion. It would not exist in every culture in varied forms and pass down through the ages of history if there wasn't a base of truth for healing abilities. Look within yourself for this energy. Let God manifest it through you and always remember to thank God for the healing and for the healer He sent if you are dealing with one.

Maria D'Andrea's Secret Occult Gallery And Spell Casting Formulary

The Out-of-Body Experience: How To Travel Without Luggage

An out-of-body experience is an experience in which your soul leaves the physical body – your soul being within your astral body form and capable of traveling anywhere. This experience is also known as astral projection; soul flight; exteriorization; OBE; or astral travel.

This is a part of human experience found throughout all cultures and history. The out-of-body experience has been recorded for all to understand and work with if one chooses to do so. These occurrences have been reported in varied situations and by various people: housewives, doctors, on Egyptian scrolls, in the spiritual histories of Africa, China, Europe, to name a few.

This experience is not influenced by religious belief as observed by the different cultural backgrounds of the people involved. Out-of –body travel can be spontaneous or preplanned, conscious or subconscious. There are some basic ways to spot an out-of-body experience:

First: Your astral body is fully aware on all your sensory levels. You can perceive the environment you are in and fully remember upon going back to your physical body. There isn't any doubt about having the experience. You can remember details and check on them if they are in your time period or in the past.

Second: At the same time, the physical body looks as though asleep or in the death state; your "real" self is not within the physical shell at the time.

Third: The two bodies are connected by what is termed the "silver cord." The silver cord is an ethereal cord or cable of energy which has elastic properties, thus enabling you to travel unlimited distances. This cord may be able to be perceived by psychics.

Fourth: During out-of-body travel the astral body can go anywhere on this planet or on foreign planets to any location.

Fifth: Also, it is not limited to time.

Sixth: The amount of time you are out-of-body can be either pre-programmed or automatic. You would feel more refreshed upon coming back to your awakened state. This experience has a long-term effect on the individual, the reason being that, once you have experienced this state, you will no longer have any doubts about the death experience as being final.

You will be aware that your physical body is not "everything," thus, there are

other states/planes available to your soul. You will be aware that your physical body is not as limited as you imagined. You "know" there is an immortal soul that is you.

Everyone has heard of out-of-body experiences in those who are very ill or in an accident. We do not always hear of those who did not have the experience due to something traumatic. Psychically, at times, the astral body can be perceived, so if you are out-of-body at a destination where there is a person sensitive to you on this level, you will most likely be aware of being recognized. Sometimes the information you bring back can be from the future, in which case you may have a better way of dealing with the situation when it occurs or can prevent it if, for example, it is an accident.

You need to remember that, if you choose to consciously astral travel, to utilize a psychic self-defense method. This is to make sure everything will stay on a positive and safe level.

Out-of-body experiences have been part of our heritage as men and women. We need only to be aware of it and consciously utilize this ability for positive purposes if choosing to develop it.

Always remember you are one with Divine Power.

Maria D'Andrea's Secret Occult Gallery And Spell Casting Formulary

Telepathy: Direct Communication

There are numerous levels of communication, some obvious, such as the written word, sign language, Morse code, verbal levels and all the other day to day usages. At the same time, there are various other levels not as obvious at first sight. One of these is the ability to communicate through thought, known as telepathy. Another is by utilizing your sense of touch, smell, visual impact, clairaudience or just a sense of "knowing." We all use some form of these abilities at one time or another.

There are different aspects of telepathy. Some people "hear" a word or sentence of information they needed for themselves or others. This is known as "clairaudience," or clear hearing. To the person who is receiving the information, I find it sounds in your head as if it was verbal. It can be very difficult to differentiate. In fact, at one time, I was in a supermarket and "heard" my younger son, Rob, ask a question. I automatically answered verbally before I remembered that he was in school. Since I was around other people, I looked around and saw that others assumed he must be in another part of the store. It at least made logical sense to other people that way.

The same situation occurred with my older son, Rick, while he was in the Navy. He was in Egypt at the time, so distance was there, but it does not make any difference. The time and distance limit is what we set.

Some people will "see" a picture in their mind, giving the information, whether in black and white or color. It does not matter. What is important is to get the information. When you consciously work with telepathy, to get the best result you need to deal with another person and discuss it prior to the attempt.

Maria D'Andrea's Secret Occult Gallery And Spell Casting Formulary

First: Decide who will send and who will receive

Second: Set a definite time and day to start. The best way is to use the same time for a week. Then switch who sends and who receives.

To start, you can be in the same room or in different locations; it does not make any difference. You both need to close your eyes and relax your physical bodies. Let go of the muscle tensions. The person sending needs to clearly visualize the information to be sent. That could be a person, scene, name, color, symbol or anything the sender can visualize strongest. Next, the sender needs to visualize the receiving person then laser beam the effect of White Light between the Third Eye to the other's Third Eye which is located in the middle of your forehead. Send the information along the beam. Do this for at least 5 minutes in the beginning. The receiver will pick up the information in the strongest method available to the receiver.

Last, but importantly, make sure you both take notes of the information sent and received. The more you practice, the better you get. Keep in mind to always stay on the Path of Light and have faith while you learn to work with your natural ability.

Maria D'Andrea's Secret Occult Gallery And Spell Casting Formulary

Spell 7

Casting Spells With Goddess Freyja

This is a Nordic Goddess. She is also connected to the Rune Casting I do for accurate, insightful Readings.

This Goddess, also called "Lady," will work with you to create a better life. She is the most magickal of the Nordic Goddesses.

Ask for her help in:

Gaining hidden wisdom

Activating your personal Power

Fertility

Sexual pleasures

Women's mysteries

Help to win in battles

Prosperity

Love

She is associated with the feathers of the falcon.

She is the embodiment of the life force.

Always remember to say Thank You.

Ghostology: Finding Unseen Forces

Ghostology has been with us for ages, although not necessarily the term. It is the study of spirits, phantoms, human-like apparitions, shadow forms and any other information relevant to the subject.

Most people are not aware, but that also includes various forms of receiving the information. One such form is the sense of smell. Certain odors may be in the area of the spirit's vicinity, such as a rose or a perfume the spirit may have worn in life, if it is one who passed on. It may be one that is an odor that is negative to the senses. People who are sensitive in this area or psychics may pick up this spirit by smell. Others who are sensitive in varied areas will pick up the spirit/ghost differently, such as the "feeling" that someone is in the room. There isn't a way to explain it, you just know. You may also sense if the ghost is male or female; positive or negative; tall or short; also young or old; any information which comes through. Many times the information will aid in helping the ghost in some way or to help identify it to release it from that particular area.

Ghostology is a study of many forms to help understand and to work with the levels not seen or known to many. Sensitive people will, in some form, be tuned in to the vibrational forces and will comprehend. However, that does not always mean that they can explain this to others. We need to simply trust our own instinct and learn to listen with our sensitivity, not just

Maria D'Andrea's Secret Occult Gallery And Spell Casting Formulary

our ears.

If you give yourself a few moments, you can look back in your life and notice how many times you "thought" you sensed something, only to logically talk yourself out of it. Now, some of that time at least was really correct if not all. Spend some time really letting yourself feel and smell and touch and sense what is around you. Close your eyes and really "know" your environment. You may be surprised at what you really find to be true.

Ghostology has become widely accepted and basically understood by the general population.

Maria D'Andrea's Secret Occult Gallery And Spell Casting Formulary

The Inner Kingdom

The answers to your problems are within your reach. Not in the future, but now.

Not only for a few people, but for all of us.

Most people tend to look for outside information to aid in their dilemmas or to improve their lives. Instead, you need time to pull in and look, listen and feel for the answer from the Christ within. When we say, "I AM GOD," what we mean metaphysically is that we are all extensions of God. As an example, visualize a ball of brilliant white light representing God. Next, millions of small balls of white light, each small ball being a soul and each soul connected by a beam of light to its source, God. Thus, we are all part of God.

To go within ourselves to solve a problem we need only to ask a question mentally and with an honest quest for truth. The answer always comes to you, even if it means you have to give it a few attempts. The solution will come to you in various forms, such as an urge to do something or a gut feeling. Sometimes you just "know." There are also times when your answer will come in your dream state. At other times, there could be an outside influence to place you in the correct location at the right time. Pay attention when you ask as to how the information comes to you and then move on it.

We all have the power to move ourselves! We are all meant to move up in our lives, not just to survive. If our earthly father takes care of us, just think how much more our heavenly Father will always be there for us.

Learn to touch base with the Inner Christ.

We all have natural talents and abilities. It could be computer knowl-

Maria D'Andrea's Secret Occult Gallery
And Spell Casting Formulary

edge, artistic ability or a warm and giving heart. Utilize it to full capacity. It is your gift to others.

When you go with your natural flow, you also increase your success. You will feel more positive and happier. If you are not sure of what your abilities are, go within and seek the answer.

Trust the Christ within and learn to seek your own counsel.

Maria D'Andrea's Secret Occult Gallery And Spell Casting Formulary

New Age Formulary

Much has been passed down by word of mouth from our ancient elders, shamans, magi, hermits and priestesses. Throughout every age there have been real practitioners of our higher inner circles who continue to remain on the Path of Divine Light. As a longtime metaphysician, I have endeavored to refine previous ancient and modern techniques, as well as bring forth some of my very special original psychic and occult tools and methods.

Therefore, the purpose is to enable beginners, students, teachers and practitioners to not only utilize these "concepts," but aid them in developing their own along the lines of a more meaningful magickal method. Often, as we do our personal research, study and meditations to continue to propel ourselves into the flooding light of the Divine Path, we find ourselves almost buried in a sea of volumes upon volumes of material which is not always short and simple to understand. So I have prepared simple technical advice that can be followed by anyone at any level. Rather than skim over several different books, why not consolidate it all into one text so that one can easily cross-reference?

We have learned and still can learn greater methods of manifesting a more creative life via candle magick, spiritual baths, love potions, and protective charms and oils, to name a few. We can certainly implement proper psychic self-defense and we may continue to reinforce our auric field or even expand it.

It is the job of each one of us, whether student or teacher, to help make our Planet Earth a spiritual paradise and physical heaven and to avoid the accumulation of debris left by negative thought projection which hinders the upward mobility of all who desire a positive prosperous and healthy

Maria D'Andrea's Secret Occult Gallery And Spell Casting Formulary

life.

This book can help us to continue that dream for all humanity. I seek to bring forth and manifest a positive life for all who desire to change and enhance our present life, to use and create, to balance ourselves NOW. There are no special short cuts, for we who remain on the Path of Divine Light have learned, through trial and error, along with a heartfelt sincerity and upright faith, to come to understand simplified proper procedures and formulae that work continuously.

As long as we are faithful, loving, truthful, strong and sincere, we can uplift ourselves, and humanity, into a greater realm of spirituality and awareness. Thus I only ask that my book be read with an open heart and open mind. You will reap great benefits. Avoid all else you will find so that you can enjoy a better life NOW.

**Maria D'Andrea's Secret Occult Gallery
And Spell Casting Formulary**

The UFO Investigator

The responsibility of an investigator is more demanding than most people are aware of. It is very important to view every aspect from different angles and recheck all information to give it credibility. It is important to make sure the facts are accurate and in as much detail as possible.

There are always those who will never be open to new information on anything which conflicts with the outlook of their own concept of how things in the universe are. We do not need to convince them. Our only goal is to do our best to get informative facts and let each individual follow their own path.

This individual is someone who is trained in investigative techniques of varied sorts. There are numerous methods available to the investigator.

One method is radiation detection. Much can be told from radiesthesiology, which is the study of radiations and their practical use. It has been found on landing spots that there is a level which is out of the normal range for that area. In most instances this is a higher level than usual. In a few instances it has been found to be lower than the area calls for. Either way, it is a deviation from the Laws of Nature.

Another of the methods utilized is mold-casting. This would be of anything unusual in the area of a suspected landing or contact sight. Then it can be checked out at a more leisurely pace. This needs to be done to certify that there wasn't a hoax being perpetrated or some normal explainable circumstance as a cause.

Photography is also a well-known method commonly used. This is not as sure as it sounds, mainly due to the ability of photographers to manipulate the film. Though experts can usually tell when a photograph has been tampered with, even they can be fooled, thus lessening the credibility of photographs. There are numerous photographs which are unexplainable on this level and are assumed to be valid.

Investigators correlate information that archaeologists have uncovered concerning cave drawings and carvings depicting futuristic looking individuals and vehicles. They also observe statues of what appears to be people dressed in space suits and paintings of beings coming from the sky found in museums.

There are stories that need to be examined of gods talking to our ancestors and giving advice and information and teaching them. The investigator needs to look at all the information available and decipher what is myth, what is potentially valid and what is the truth. This is not a matter of simply looking at facts, but of researching for years in many instances.

Sometimes people confuse the UFO investigators with the Ufologists. A Ufologist is a person who studies, scientifically, all the aspects of outer space with a non-biased outlook. This is a field that deserves much credit. It does not look for confirmation either way on UFO activity, neither crediting nor discrediting the sightings unless it is validated in the circumstances of their search in their field.

UFO imprints have been talked about abundantly. These are circular patterns in the ground that people attribute to UFO landings; some are frauds, and some have never been explained on a satisfactory level.

There are also people who have stated that they have witnessed UFO landings or made contact with other beings. One such friend of mine is a chief of a Native American tribe. He saw the space ship land at a distance from him while traveling on a road in a van. He was with friends at the time who also saw the ship. He said when the ship was sighted by him, the van stopped and he wanted to get out and to meet the beings on the ship to exchange information and to learn from each other. He said it did not occur to him to be afraid. In his outlook on life there is Oneness with nature, of all life forms having common ground. However, the others he was with prevented him from getting out of the vehicle, not having the same outlook. Maybe we are not all prepared for this contact, but at least some are. The way is becoming more and more open as time goes by. The chief is some-

Maria D'Andrea's Secret Occult Gallery
And Spell Casting Formulary

one the investigators would be interested in questioning.

As we become more open to new thoughts and ideas, we will find a vast diversification of abilities and talents on this planet, as well as others. Look for the signs with an open mind, heart and spiritual awareness. Remember we are all one with Divine Power, and each other.

Maria D'Andrea's Secret Occult Gallery And Spell Casting Formulary

Spell 8

To Bring In Luck

Bring luck to you easily. Do this on a Sunday. First, focus your intent on repeating frequently- "I am always lucky."

It doesn't matter if you believe it or not. Just put it out in the Word or thought.

With a green pen, draw a picture of a horseshoe and draw seven little lines in it to represent where nails go. Sprinkle the paper with a little alfalfa or chamomile herb. Carry this with you at all times, in your wallet or close to your body.

Hobgoblins

Many people have heard of the Hobgoblin and some as children listened to stories about them on a negative level; children's stories to keep them in line, story-telling for fun, but nonetheless scary.

Myths, tales and stories coming down the line through generations, retold so often and in varied ways that at times it is forgotten that there was ever a truth that they were based upon.

Hobgoblins are nature spirits. They are also more familiarly known as Goblins. Some people, such as psychics or people who are sensitive to the non-physical realms, can see them. Sometimes you may be more open to your psychic levels.

These nature spirits are really fairies. However, fairies have numerous categories, which is mainly due to people needing to label and identify in this manner to clarify for themselves.

The name Goblin is given to the spirits that are more mischievous.

These nature spirits are on a lower mentality level and thus are also unreasonable. If one is in your home area and you make contact, this is not a spirit you could explain your situation to and ask it to leave. You would need to make it a command for it to have any effect.

Hobgoblins like to make contact and be seen, when possible, on a psychic, clairvoyant level. This is due to the mischievous attitude and the spirit having fun and delight in causing surprise, unsettlement or chaos. Sometimes these spirits are also known to be shape-shifters, thus, they can appear on and off as animals or thieves, among other forms. These nature spirits are also known for their small, heavyset bodies and round looking

Maria D'Andrea's Secret Occult Gallery
And Spell Casting Formulary

countenance or scary looks. Although at times these Hobgoblins are dealing from negative aspects, they can be minor troublemakers.

All spirit is under our control. Being in the physical body, we all have free will over spirits. Thus, any spirit that you may come into contact with and do not want around, you can control it having to leave. Simply state as a command that the spirit has to leave now. State that you are commanding this through the Power of God, Buddha or whoever to you is Divine Power. Keep repeating this on and off until the spirit leaves – and it will, since it does not have control. You do.

When hearing myths or legends you can look into them more and find the base cause or truth that it grew from. There are numerous nature spirits and the Hobgoblin is only one form of them. Think of them more as a mischievous fairy.

Maria D'Andrea's Secret Occult Gallery And Spell Casting Formulary

Ghosts Of The Tribes

All our modern day activities and hectic running around still leave our sensitivities open to the past and to the spirit world. This is as it should be. When you are psychic, intuitive or sensitive, it is as though you are walking on a tightrope between the two realities. One side is the astral plane, spirit, and the other is the physical plane; we are meant to deal with both equally. Ghosts are found in varied environments and much more frequently than supposed. You need only to leave yourself open and pay attention, not from your intellect, but from your sensitivity levels.

A few years ago, while I was on vacation, I was in a car on the highway. It was dusk, and we sped along looking at the scenery. I noticed further in the front of us Native Americans walking back and forth crossing the highway. First I thought it was strange that the cars kept missing them and I could not understand why they picked that particular area to cross. As we moved closer, I realized they were not solid, but slightly translucent. It was difficult not to cringe as we drove through a female figure. We stopped and contacted a spirit. If you ask questions, there are frequent times that they are answered.

Apparently the highway ran through old Indian tribal ground. It was very peaceful and serene. Just as tribal everyday occurrences had gone on in life, now they continued on another plane. The cars and modern day activities went by unnoticed.

The Native Americans, although on the next plane of existence, still felt the connection between themselves and nature blending with the forces of the universe and the laws of nature, utilizing them and accepting the forces as being one with them.

Maria D'Andrea's Secret Occult Gallery And Spell Casting Formulary

There is much to be gained by contacting these spirits and asking questions to put perspective to our way of life living with Mother Earth and all of the elements. We have them at our disposal to be used as a positive power. We need only tune into a source we can communicate with.

We, in the physical body, have all the controls. We have free will that governs the spirits on the other side. They are bound by Divine Providence to answer our questions or leave. However, you must always remember to use a form of psychic protection prior to contact to be safe, such as prayer. Use your sensitivities to be more aware of your surroundings and to tune into both reality levels. Look around, feel, sense and listen. Trust your own intuitive input. You may be surprised at what you tune into and gain as information. Try going to areas known for being old Native American sites, as they are very psychically synchronized with us. Just stay quiet and open and let all of your senses be open.

Take a notebook with you and write down everything. This will give you a reference point at a later date. Remember to use psychic protection and have fun.

Maria D'Andrea's Secret Occult Gallery And Spell Casting Formulary

The Tidra
(A Children's Story)

Hidden deep in the emerald green forest among the giant ferns there was a peaceful glen at a time when the world was still young and elves roamed Mother Earth. There lived beautiful, slender golden elves that called themselves the Tidra. They dressed in the clothes provided by nature, bright colored tunics and pants of yellow, orange and green leaves. Dresses of leaves with shimmering spider webs for decoration.

The Tidra were always singing and dancing, flickering between the trees that were their homes, and if you look very closely you can see there is a bright white light within all of them. They know just as we do that we are all sparks of the same white light.

Two of the elves, Elysian and Orion, were busy playing with the Tidra's pet dragon called Firelight, a rare, golden dragon who loved to fly in the dark night sky lit by the specks of bright stars, to stretch his golden, leathery wings and feel the wind rushing past. He loved to let his breath of fire blaze across the blackness, but most of all, he loved to share his feelings of joy with his friends as he soared with an elf upon his neck.

One clear, sunny day Orion found a bright quartz crystal gleaming behind a bush. You could see the light shining through it. It was the most beautiful thing the elf ever saw. Orion quickly went to show it to the other elves. "Look, everyone, look! I have a wonderful treasure!" And all the elves gathered around him. One of the other elves said, "Please let me hold it. I just want to see how it feels." And he held out his thin elfin hand. After all, the elves know everything comes from the same place, from God. He provides for all our needs. Everything that comes from the earth belongs to us

Maria D'Andrea's Secret Occult Gallery And Spell Casting Formulary

all, so it is natural to share. But to all the elves' surprise, Orion closed his hand over the crystal and said, "NO." It was very unexpected. Then he walked away by himself. As he came to a nearby tree he sat down under it and realized he was truly tired. As though the crystal knew what Orion was feeling, the crystal started to glow more and more, then it passed healing energy into Orion. Soon he was feeling much better, more like his happy, singing self.

As he was trying to figure out what happened, Firelight walked towards him. He seemed so sad, not like himself at all. "Hello, Firelight," called Orion. "Why are you so sad? Maybe we could go flying together. That always cheers you up."

"No thank you," said Firelight. "There is something wrong with me and I don't know what to do. I can't breathe fire anymore and what is a fire dragon without his fire?" Then he walked away looking very unhappy.

Orion thought and thought. If he let Firelight hold his crystal, maybe he would get well. But that would mean he would have to share, and after all, what if it does not help Firelight at all and just takes all the energy from his special crystal? Orion thought, "Maybe he will just get better on his own." He knew in his heart thought that Firelight was not getting any better at all.

The next day he went to look for the Tidra's dragon. Orion found him curled up at the base of a tree, his large wings enfolding him. "Do you feel better today?" asked Orion.

"No, and I am getting more and more tired. If this keeps up I may not even be able to fly."

Firelight had such a sad unhappy voice.

Orion thought of how much the elves all loved their pet dragon. All the fun they had soaring above the clouds and how happy the dragon made all of them. Firelight never expected anything in return. He did it out of love from his big heart.

Shyly, since Orion knew he should have offered it before, he held his hand out with the crystal gleaming brightly in his palm.

"I am not sure this will help you Firelight, but it helped me when I was tired. Maybe if you hold it, the crystal will also help you." Then he added, "It doesn't really matter if you will use it all up as you get well."

Firelight thanked the elf and took the crystal.

As soon as Firelight had it, the crystal began to glow brighter and brighter, and as it glowed, Firelight felt better and better. Finally he tested his wings and then his fire breath. Everything was back to normal. He was so very happy. He thanked Orion for being so unselfish as he gave the crystal back. Orion took it, expecting it to be dull now with all its energy gone. To his surprise, it was glowing brighter, stronger and more beautiful than ever. All of a sudden Orion remembered his mother telling him when he was just a little elf, "The more you give from your heart, the more you get back." Only now he understood what she meant; that we have an endless supply of love and everything else to give.

They were both so excited that they went on a happy flight and to this day, now and then, when you look into the night sky, you may see a speck darting between the clouds and hear happy laughter in the still of the night.

Maria D'Andrea's Secret Occult Gallery And Spell Casting Formulary

The Link Between Realities

Numerous people go to church each week and do not take the time to converse with God any other time, not only through prayer but also through meditation.

Meditation is the link between the two Realities, physical and spiritual. When you spend a few moments of your time in silence, you open yourself to a world of information, spiritual enlightenment and inner peace, harmony and balance. Relax your body and mind, feel the God force within instead of looking outward, allow your muscles to relax and let go. Your tensions of the day, your problems, are put on the side.

Say to yourself, "Be still and know that God's within me." Let your mind dwell on it and absorb it. Feel the stillness with all your being.

Know that you are part and one of God. He is always there for you, at all times, and all places. He loves all of us and wants our happiness. Meditation is our way of direct contact with God, our source.

When you have a problem, ask how to solve it in your meditation, then listen to the indwelling Lord; that voice within us all. You will get an answer. Remember Matthew 7:7 – "Ask and it will be given you; seek and you will find; knock and it will be opened to you."

Sometimes it may take two to three tries but you will get an answer you are meant to receive.

Let yourself relax and use your meditation abilities to aid you in your life; to help direct you to the right Path. You need only to be open to it and then use your free will to decide how to utilize the information to move ahead.

God is there for you every day, not just one or two days of the week.

Maria D'Andrea's Secret Occult Gallery And Spell Casting Formulary

The advice within may not be spoken out loud but you will hear it just the same. You may see or hear something psychically or get a gut feeling or urge to do something, or you may even just know what to do. The Bible says "Peace! Be still!" in Mark 4:39. Don't just read these words. Follow them!

Ask, listen and then move on it.

Move on the information you have received, don't just settle for getting it. You need to use it for it to be of any help. You stand on a tight rope when you meditate in between the two worlds of God and Man.

Listen with your heart, mind and soul. Go with the infinite wisdom then follow that voice to improve your life on all levels. Health, love, finance, romance, work and anything else you may need to work on.

The power is yours. Utilize it NOW.

**Maria D'Andrea's Secret Occult Gallery
And Spell Casting Formulary**

Story Of The Bats
(A Children's Story)

Once upon a time the bats were the most beautiful creatures on earth. The parrots did not have such magnificently colored dresses, the peacocks such glittering crowns, the nightingales such sweet voices as the bats had at one time. They so enjoyed their lives, flying in the warm sunshine, jumping around in the flowery meadows.... And when the other animals heard them sing, they all listened enraptured and quietly.

They lived this way for a long time until the wicked fairies, the willies, got envious of their happiness. They just did not like to see them so happy day in and day out.

It was late one night and the trees were bowing their heads in the darkness and there were no bright stars in the sky, when from the deep center of the earth hundreds and thousands of willies started to fly towards the nests of the sleeping bats. The bats did not feel any danger. They slept peacefully. The willies jumped hurriedly one after the other into the nests, grabbed the brilliant clothing, the shimmering crowns, even their sweet voices were taken from their throats. They were left with only some gray, dirty pieces of cloth, two brown leather wings and very, very ugly little faces. When all was done, these wicked fairies flew back laughing and shrieking all the way home.

The sun was just rising on the horizon when the bats woke up. All of a sudden there was so much commotion, running, looking for their lost items and their voices. They just could not imagine what had happened. They flew to the birds and asked them politely, "Can you help us, little birds, little friends? We cannot find our beautiful dresses, our crowns, all our fortune is gone."

"Who are you, what are you?" asked the birds. The way the poor bats looked they could not be recognized by anyone.

"We are bats and we do not know who or why, but someone, at night, stole all our belongings" said the bats. Can you imagine though? The birds did not believe them.

"Ugly animals, disappear from here this instant. Do not come near us. Do not live near us." And they flew away.

So they turned to the other animals until they talked to all of them but none recognized the beautiful bats in their new gray and brown ugly appearance. Poor, poor bats! By now they were very tired and sad. It was nightfall approaching by this time and none of the trees and shrubs were ready to give them shelter. They flew on and on, further and further away until they came upon a cave. There were even some small cracks in the rocky mountainside. Some of them crawled into those and slept, others continued on until they saw a large ruin of a castle ahead.

"What shall we do?" They argued and discussed it back and forth until some of them took courage and flew inside the ruins. And what did they see? Thousands of willies were dancing in the tower in the darkness. They all were enveloped in gorgeous bat-clothing with glittering crowns on their heads, their songs were so absolutely beautiful and heartwarming that the bats listening to them were so overcome that they just listened and listened ..... All of a sudden one of the fairies discovered them and in one second they all ran in a thousand different directions and disappeared in the darkness.

The bats were so tired by now. They were sad, but mostly hungry. They started to catch insects and night moths for their dinner because there was nothing else around to eat. Later, when dawn arose they returned to the castle. They grabbed the beams with their feet and immediately fell asleep hanging upside down. This way, even in their dreams, they could watch the tower and the grounds for the fairies' return.

Since those times, when the last rays of sun disappeared on the horizon, the poor bats start to wake up and start to chase the night insects to collect food. Late at night in every ruin, in every old castle, in caves and crannies they are awake and are watching for the return of the willies when they start their dancing.

All this is not helping them because at midnight their songs float on the air and the bats, forgetting their plight, just listen to their voices. After a while some of them try to fly to the tower to get back their belongings, but all they can see is the willies disappearing in the depths of the earth.

Maria D'Andrea's Secret Occult Gallery And Spell Casting Formulary

Maria D'Andrea's Secret Occult Gallery And Spell Casting Formulary

Spell 9

The Spell Of Love

Love spells from ancient times often utilize apples. These were thought of in Wiccan, as well as in other religions, as vibrational/magnetic frequencies for working with love.

The power of the apple is connected to feminine energies. And thus, to Deities such as:
Venus
Aphrodite
Diana
Hera
Dionysus
Isis
Athena

The energy of water, which deals with emotions, is also at play here.

The best day for this spell to be created is on a Friday or Sunday.

To make a love sachet, take some apple blossoms and combine them with an emerald, rose quartz, turquoise or Arizona Agate stone.

Add to this a sigil:

On white paper, with black ink, write the name of one of the Deities above, then focus on what your intent is. For example: true love, positive relationship, marriage, long term relationship. Always focus on "this or better," in case the Universal energies have a better plan for you.

Once the sachet is sewn (or you can pin it closed), put a drop of either Love Oil or Success Oil on it, as you refocus your intent.

Carry this with you at all times and remember to look for it, expect it, trust that it is coming to you. After all, if you don't expect it to come, why would it?

**Maria D'Andrea's Secret Occult Gallery
And Spell Casting Formulary**

Story About Earth: How Did the Earth Become A Brilliant Star? (A Children's Story)

Millions and billions of twinkling stars dotted the skies and God was enjoying watching them proudly. All of a sudden a small, dark, colorless star came in front of God's throne, stopped and said in a tearful, complaining voice, "My Lord, I am the Earth...", but he could not continue because he was choking on his tears.

"What is the problem? What is wrong, little earth?" asked God, being friendly.

"Ah, great injustice was done to me, my Lord! All my star brothers and sisters are bright and shining with brilliance, only I have stayed colorless and drab."

God shook his head in consternation and called on Archangel Michael. "What has happened here, Michael?" He asked. "I have trusted you with the care of all the stars; you are supposed to make sure that all are shining brightly. Now, we have this poor little earth who has stayed dark."

Michael bowed his head and asked for forgiveness.

"Dear Lord, please forgive me this time because I have truly forgotten about the earth."

"That is not right, Michael" said God very seriously. "You see, much injustice was done to this star named earth. You know well that I cannot just forget about an act like this. You must think hard and come up with a plan to correct your mistake."

Naturally, Michael tried to come up with an idea but he was not lucky, although he concentrated for three days and three nights. Then he asked the angels to help him. Needless to say, the angels could not help him to get the earth shining brightly. Finally he stood again in front of God and told him what was happening.

"All right, my son, I will help you this one time, but be careful that others should not suffer because of your forgetfulness. Hear what I have decided upon."

By this time all the angels and all the stars surrounded God and listened with great interest.

"I will have men to be born on earth," said the Lord, "Men who will be different and much more superior to any of my other creatures. I will form them after my own image and I will give them part of my own soul. The star, named Earth, is now dark and colorless but as soon and as often as MEN will produce something noble, something good, appropriate to his eternal soul, each of those times the Earth will get lighter. You will see, Michael and all of you angels, that one time soon the Earth will shine more brilliantly and with warmer colors than any of the other stars in the sky. You just wait patiently until the souls of men will brighten this drab, poor star."

And, it so happened that our Earth is getting brighter and brighter until one day the words of God will come true. The good, true and noble deeds of men will miraculously change our planet, the star of Earth, to the most beautiful, brilliant star.

**Maria D'Andrea's Secret Occult Gallery
And Spell Casting Formulary**

Empowerment Through The Word

In our fast rushing society, most people look to the outside for success. Success in all areas of life, each individual in search of varied needs. People look for courses, directions from those who teach, they go to seminars, workshops, study groups. Now, all of these are fine and are there to aid those who choose to take advantage of them, however, there is a simpler, more direct way to set your goals and achieve your needs and dreams.

There is literally Power in the Word.

One of the best ways to utilize this power source is to first decide what your goals are. This can be achieved through a period of quiet, by listening to your inner self. Let yourself feel the direction to go in, go within to touch your source, your Higher Self. Your first intuition sense will be correct.

Next, use your Bible to aid in your quest. The Psalms are the best for this purpose. They attract or repel, depending on what you are working towards, such as attracting a new job or repelling a negative situation that has been blocking your progress. Look through the Psalms and focus on what you desire. You will find the correct one for your purpose.

Next, repeat the Psalm at least once per day, keeping focused and knowing you will achieve results. As an example:

If you need to attract prosperity in business, repeat Psalm #122 during business hours frequently. Lighting a green or orange candle at the location site would also help. If you do not have the time to read the whole Psalm, at least read through it once, then the rest of the time repeat just verse #7.

To attract Divine Grace, repeat Psalm #103 from the heart. As with the Psalm, if you want it to work you need to be sincere.

Maria D'Andrea's Secret Occult Gallery And Spell Casting Formulary

To heighten self-confidence and business, repeat Psalm #108 prior to going to work. This Psalm will also give you a more positive attitude on Life.

The Word was meant to be used, not just looked at, read and dismissed.

What you can conceive, you can achieve. Focus on the power of the Word and rekindle your desires and goals, for as you do so, you will already be receiving your answer.

**Maria D'Andrea's Secret Occult Gallery
And Spell Casting Formulary**

Influence Of UFO's On Spiritual Awareness

The UFO's influence has been with us for centuries on the spiritual level. There are numerous situations we are knowledgeable of, more so in the metaphysical field.

In the time of the cave paintings, we come across art depicting human forms with what looks as though they are wearing space helmets. This has been well documented. For people who are not highly advanced, this would have left a spiritual impression, more on the level of miracles of what the visitors may have been able to accomplish compared to themselves rather than having the effect to seek new knowledge of how to put the "astronaut's" abilities to practical use.

In ancient times they had the High Priestess wear a copper band with a terminated clear quartz crystal placed on the front about where the Third Eye would be located, the point towards the sky. She would then go up on a high hill or mountain and with her arms outstretched go into a form of trance state to send and receive information for her people, the band being a form of transmitter. This band was constructed as a form of communication system to a distant home planet, the theory being that one or several UFOs landed and used this method to keep in touch with their home. When their ships went back to their planet they left this form of keeping in touch.

As time went by, people forgot the original purpose and started using it as worship, with the High Priestess going through the same physical motions and waiting for an answer, not knowing really from where, which never came. As the ritual was passed down from one High Priestess to the next, somewhere the reason was diffused and lost to most.

Some people, to this day, construct their own band and try to communicate with other life forces in the distant sky.

Many psychics have a different view of UFOs. They are not questioning if they exist. They already do. Some psychics have an interest in what course of action happens concerning the UFO activities and even communicate with other living forms with a soul-mind. We can gain information to aid our people and planet and learn to escalate and elevate our progress on a spiritual level.

Occultists are also aware. However, few would have a strong interest in this form of travel for themselves. Occultists, as a whole, prefer out-of-body travel. Nevertheless, since they are able to choose their destination, they can contact UFOs and other intelligences, as well as other contacts on the astral plane.

Maria D'Andrea's Secret Occult Gallery And Spell Casting Formulary

Voodoo Dolls: Ancient Tools For Modern Man

Numerous types of dolls have always been with us for varied spiritual purposes. These dolls can be utilized for positive or negative petitions, the energy worked with being neutral and the practitioner directing its use as one or the other. It is a very real force and should be used only for good, remembering that what you put out in word or thought will also come back to you. Only positive, only positive!!!

Their use is not limited or more dominant in any particular culture. In some countries it may be more "underground," in some, more open. West Africa, Haiti or the West Indies are more open and known for Voodoo dolls. The word Voodoo means "God." Their use is also very prevalent in Europe, such as Hungary. Russians and Native Americans are also well known for this practice. In Guatemala, even the children put them to conscious work.

Voodoo dolls are very commonplace. In Voodoo practice you choose a doll to represent the person you want to work on, male or female. You can also do work for yourself. Next, attach something belonging to the individual to the doll, such as hair, part of a shirt or anything personal.

You are now building empathy or what we call "sympathetic magick." This is similar to the scientific principle of cause and effect and the religious outlook of "As above, so below."

As you work with the doll, you put all your thoughts of what you want done and all your emotions into it. Never deviate from your purpose. Make it POSITIVE! You can aid others through a financial crisis, help speed up the healing process, or anything that will help that particular situation.

You place the doll where it will not be touched by others or seen. You do not want their thoughts or negative energy to counteract your petition.

Maria D'Andrea's Secret Occult Gallery And Spell Casting Formulary

Dolls can be made of material, clay or any form you feel comfortable with, clay being the ancient method.

Witches carried the dolls for religious reasons in the jungle to represent the Goddess. The doll was to be placed on their altar. Children carried them as imitation, originally. Later, as a way to adjust to society, in practicing.

In Guatemala, they carry Trouble Dolls. They are also known as Blessing Dolls. These are six (6) small dolls initially used in occult practices. Later, they were carried over to be utilized by the children. The Indians teach that you share your troubles with the dolls. Utilize one doll for each problem. Prior to going to sleep, tell the doll your trouble. While you are sleeping, it will work to solve it for you. This is a very good focus point and as you concentrate on your problem, you will know the outcome to be positive.

In Hungary, the Voodoo dolls are used by Shamans as an aid to healing and attracting your needs. Numerous times they are utilized in conjunction with herbs, oils or candles. They are an integral part of the Hungarian Shamans' work.

Dolls are very powerful ancient tools and should be considered as such. Previous to any Spiritual work, meditate on your purpose to be sure you are doing positive work. Ask Divine Power for guidance. When you make your petition, put all your energy into it, "knowing you are positive." Utilize this tool to help yourself and others. Remember to walk in the Path of Light …..

Maria D'Andrea's Secret Occult Gallery And Spell Casting Formulary

We Are The Law Of Abundance Manifest

People look to the outside in search of their riches. Their prosperity on all levels: emotional, financial, health, love and spiritual. Yet many times they search in vain.

Have you ever wondered why some people are always living in abundance, while others go through constant poverty? The ones who are living in abundance are aware of one simple fact – that money is not your goal and your supply; your only supply is God.

Your life is an outward picture of your inner belief. If you believe you do not deserve money, do not work hard enough for it, opportunities are not there or negate it in some way, then it will never come to you on the level you want it to. On the other hand, if you "know" the opposite to be true, then you will manifest the situation you want.

Money is not your goal. It is a tool to utilize towards improving your life. You may want a better house for your family or a better car to get to your job. More money enables you to be of more help to numerous people and to help improve your environment. As you make more money, you need to help others to elevate those in need, perhaps through spiritual guidance, not necessarily with money. WE are abundance in action!

Visualize that you are One with God, part of God and as such you are a co-creator. This creative energy flows through you and the substance creates whatever you want in your life. This energy of spiritual love flows into you, through you, surrounds you and flows out from you to form what your mind and emotions tell it. Trust it. You are the energy that manifests.

If you believed in lack, in disappointments or in being alone, make the decision right now to stop. Start "knowing" that is not real. You do not

Maria D'Andrea's Secret Occult Gallery
And Spell Casting Formulary

have to work hard at getting what you want. You just need to be aware of the Law of Abundance and how it functions. Let your spiritual self manifest for you, not your physical self. Keep an eye out for opportunities and work with positive attitudes, honesty and love.

If you have an urge to do something, do it.

When you are aware of the fact that you are the one manifesting, information and new openings to various situations will come to you. You need only to work with them.

Remember, you are working on both realities: physical and non-physical. The only job you have is to know the Truth and each day focus on it for a few minutes. The Bible says, "And the Lord will guide you continually, and satisfy your desire with good things." Isaiah 58:11.

Know that God within you manifests all your needs. You are his child and he wants you to be happy. It is your Divine birthright. Allow it to happen. Let your awareness be your open door to abundance.

**Maria D'Andrea's Secret Occult Gallery
And Spell Casting Formulary**

Dreams: Your Direct Phone Line

People tend to look at dreams as possible escapes, informative at times, or they simply ignore them. Few people actually utilize this vast source of energy that is always easily available to them.

You can use dreams to answer questions for you, to aid in your spiritual, material, emotional and physical growth. To gain knowledge on what to do in any situation you run across.

In Matthew 7:7, it says in the Bible, "Ask and you will receive, seek and you will find, knock and the door will be opened to you."

One of the methods you can use is dream work.

Before you go to sleep, consciously think of the situation you want resolved. If you need to know how someone really feels, or how an important business deal will go and how to improve the outcome, or where to look for your right relationship, this method will give you the answer. If you need to, then visualize the scene in your mind, or just mentally ask your question a few times. Then go to sleep. Relax. The answer will come.

It is as though you picked up the phone and asked a friend for information. Just as with a friend, you may not get an immediate response. They may need to check into the situation and later come back with the answer. So, if you do not get your answer the first night, do the dream work again the following night.

Usually you will get an answer by the third night of dream work.

However, there are times when you should not know the answer. At various points in your life, it could be a karmic situation that needs to be resolved, or the timing is wrong so you will get your answer at a later date.

Maria D'Andrea's Secret Occult Gallery
And Spell Casting Formulary

Prior to sleep, ask for the answer to be understandable to you.

You want an answer that makes sense to you. If you get a response in numbers, it would not make sense to you unless you are a numerologist. It will not help you if you do not have any connection to the information you receive.

In Genesis 40:89 it tells us that, "It is God who gives the ability to interpret dreams." You are asking for the help to interpret your dreams correctly. Make sure you ask for a positive purpose, such as solving a disagreement. If you cannot agree with a friend, you can ask how your friend really feels. If you understand your friend's point of view, you will be able to resolve it faster.

Use the dream work for helping you to succeed in all your life paths. …. Always remember your Source and have fun with it.

Maria D'Andrea's Secret Occult Gallery And Spell Casting Formulary

Maria D'Andrea's Secret Occult Gallery And Spell Casting Formulary

Spell 10

The Whim Of The Gods Spell

Granting wishes was one of the wonderful abilities of the Gods (Deities). We are all in the process of moving now from the *Fourth Dimensional* ways (Desires) to the *Fifth Dimensional* way of thought (Manifesting quickly). This means that now, as you are focusing on what your intent is to bring into this reality, it is already doing so.

To tap into this powerful Source, do the following:

Focus on what you wish to be creating and to see coming into your life. Then ask the angel Donel, who is one of the guardians of the gates of the South Wind, and the Deity known as Odin, to hear you and work with you in a positive way only, and to now manifest what your intent is by saying:

I am now protected through the Power of the Divine,

I now call forth the Power of Odin to be my supply.

I now call forth the South Gate, Donel

Bring to me what I desire.

My desire is (FILL IN YOUR DESIRE).

Thank you, for as I ask, I receive.

So Be It.

Maria D'Andrea's Secret Occult Gallery And Spell Casting Formulary

Dream Pillows

You have chosen to join us on this night to honor your Dreamtime and to "birth" …not only your Dream Pillow, but also your wanting to join with Spirit, Earth Mother and the energies around us to encourage your dreams and visions…a doorway to your inner self. As you learn about the different "medicines," we encourage you to select those that you feel comfortable with. For this evening we have chosen to share some that are known for their "Dream Connections," as well as others that we will teach you about.

From Earth Mother's Plant Kingdom we have:

Lavender: which brings a sense of calmness and helps to manifest inner strength and courage. It is connected to the vibration of empowerment. This herb is especially powerful for women at times of stress and as they cycle through menstruation, childbirth and menopause.

Mugwort: is ruled by the Goddess Artemis, Goddess of the Moon, who legend says used her plants for healing animals, warriors, women and children Mugwort is known for its ability to stimulate dreams and to help you as you travel in the dreamtime.

Rose Petals: attract love and are often blended with other herbs to surround them with a gentle loving energy.

Valerian Root: is soothing and calming and known for its "medicine" of rest and peaceful sleep.

Yarrow: is an "overall tonic" and is used for "attraction. It is present in the south in the medicine wheel and can help to open the doors to trust, innocence and abundance.

Copal: is a resin that has a powerful connection with the spirit and medicine of women. It is used to cleanse and "call" to our ancestors for teachings and guidance.

And from the Mineral Kingdom we have ....

Herkimer Diamonds: which will enhance your "cosmic" connection. They are known for their ability to "amplify" energy and increase your awareness of your dreams.

Jade: will assist you with releasing your emotions and remembering your dreams. Jade radiates the energy of spirit and unconditional love.

Opal: has been used to invoke visions and "happy dreams." It is connected with enhancing intuition and connecting you with your Higher Self.

Moonstone: is the stone for "hoping and wishing" and for enhancing feelings and intuition. It truly holds and enhances the feminine energy.

**Maria D'Andrea's Secret Occult Gallery
And Spell Casting Formulary**

God's Creatures – A Psychic Connection

Have you ever noticed how animals are drawn to certain people? However, that does not mean that the person likes them. It is simply that this individual has psychic energy. Animals can sense this and are drawn to it.

We are all creatures of God. All animals, including man, have psychic ability.

All species of animals have an inborn awareness of the intention of other animals, plants, nature and, of course, man's sensitivities. This ability is for survival. We are all aware of animals sensing danger before it hits. We have all had a feeling at one time or another of sensing someone walking behind us. This is the survival instinct.

Some of us have a stronger psychic connection to animals than others. There is a strong empathy link. Usually this is an inborn ability.

Animal trainers are usually gifted. They control animals through psychic means. Not a negative control, but giving off a psychic feeling of harmony, balance and empathy with the animal, which the animal picks up. The animal will feel safe and trust the person, "knowing" it will not be harmed. We have seen tamers at the circus dealing with a lion without a weapon.

Conscious use of this ability can be utilized for positive purposes such as on a farm. It may be overrun by rabbits to the detriment of the crops. A farmer with this ability can ask them to move off the property by telepathy. They will leave, without being killed.

Mystics and occult workers also utilize this link consciously. When needed, we can draw upon the animal qualities. When backed into a corner, some people react like a lion. It is not a conscious choice. However, a psychic could draw on these qualities deliberately and utilize them to the full potential. Lions being brave, protective, with strong survival and family instincts, do this well and are a good choice.

The snake has been with us for untold ages in myths, stories and the Bible. In some religions, such as the snake cults, the snake is used in ritual work. They believe that if they have enough faith in God, then handling a poisonous snake is safe. They will then attain higher consciousness, such as psychic abilities and healing powers.

Maria D'Andrea's Secret Occult Gallery And Spell Casting Formulary

Psychic Rune Casting To American Indian Crafts (Example Of Positive Psychics At Their Work)

I have always been concerned about fakes in the field. They do us all a disservice and hurt our credibility tremendously. Some years ago I did a press release about this which I think is worth repeating here. Read it as if I were just making these statements now.

In a field which we acknowledge is plagued with fakes, there are some psychics who have a high code of ethics and deal on a professional level.

On March 5, 1989, Rev. Maria D'Andrea (now Solomon) will be presenting a Psychic Fair located at the African Poetry Theatre, 176-03 Jamaica Ave., Jamaica, NY 11433 held from 11:00 a.m. – 6:00 p.m. Three will be a $3 admission charge.

Psychic readers and other experts in the metaphysical field will be available for readings and consultation.

The Director of Operations for the Psychic Fair, Richard, said, "All the readers have been screened for this Psychic Fair and are well-known in their field. Rev. Maria is an author who has been doing psychic readings, rune casting and varied spiritual work for over twenty years. WLIB radio listeners will be pleased to hear that Top Numerologist Lloyd Strayhorn will be among the readers."

The psychics selected for this Fair utilize varied tools such as clairvoyance, palmistry, tarot cards, psychometry, Kirlian photography and American Indian cards to name a few. Each reader varies.

As Rev. Maria always says: "The information given by a psychic is meant to be used as a guide. If something is not going well in your life, you

Maria D'Andrea's Secret Occult Gallery
And Spell Casting Formulary

will be told. However, you will also be told why it is not working so you can use your free will to turn the situation around."

In addition to the readers, there will also be a number of vendors with a wide range of metaphysical products displayed for sale. Many of these products are almost impossible to get through normal channels. All of the vendors are spiritual and knowledgeable.

The March 5th Psychic Fair is the first of a series of Fairs planned by Rev. Maria, all being of the same high quality and standards.

Maria D'Andrea's Secret Occult Gallery And Spell Casting Formulary

Universal Lines Of Force

Known by various names such as Ley Lines and Dragon Lines, these lines of force are understood and can be utilized. These are energy lines through the universe and a path of power extending through and around the world. Some are marked on the earth's surface by giant structures built thousands of years ago.

The pyramids, Stonehenge and various megalithic sites have unexplained properties where the Ley Lines intersect.

The energy can be seen and felt by some people such as psychics and martial artists. They can also be found by various methods, such as dowsing for them.

When you are at a point where the lines intersect, the power and force is magnified. These power spots can heighten your rituals and energy. They are said to be utilized for building portals to other dimensions. They are also used to pull energy into yourself for attaining a positive goal of healing yourself or others.

These lines of force create a geometrical and planetary grid. They are uniformly spaced, which creates horizontal and vertical force fields. One should keep in mind an old axiom which states "as above, so below." This means that we have the same type of grid patterns within the physical body. These are commonly known as Chakra Energy Centers, Acupuncture Meridians and Reflexology points.

Keeping all this in mind, we can now understand how we all can be affected by universal lines of force. We are all connected as one unity. Therefore, we as the microcosm are united with the macrocosm.

Maria D'Andrea's Secret Occult Gallery And Spell Casting Formulary

Tree Doctor

In the cool deepness of a green forest

Stands a stately oak tree.

So many little birds are nesting

On its large branches under shady leaves.

Do you know why the birds are so sad today,

None are chirping, singing cheerful songs?

Their landlord, the ancient oak, suffers

Greatly and for a long time.

He is weak because of the unbearable pain

Inflicted on him.

Vivacious insects use his sweet juice

For their drink and food.

From high above in the sky the sun looks down,

Sending warm rays deep into the forest.

Meanwhile plans are in the making by

The inhabitants of the old oak tree.

They skip from branch to branch in a hurry

To get together to help their friend and landlord

"Where is the doctor?' they chirp and sing in unison.

Maria D'Andrea's Secret Occult Gallery And Spell Casting Formulary

Just then the good doctor Woodpecker

Flies into their midst.

The Tree Doctor walks up and down, checking,

Working as he knocks and hammers constantly.

Finally he finds deep holes in the bark and

Calls out joyously

"I have got you, you mean, mean enemy!"

What and who are the troublemakers?

Insects, they are the ones and urgently he

Tries to get rid of the uninvited guests.

Repeating all along the way: "Go away and

Stay away! You are not needed here!

Leave our mighty oak tree alone!"

And so it happened that the life of the sweet,

Beautiful oak was saved and very soon

His wounds will heal.

He will cover each and every small nest

With his softly rustling leaves and happy,

Joyous songs will float up high towards the Sun,

Then fully from all the little birds, even the

Raccoons, squirrels and all the animals of

The green forest chimed in gratefully.

Maria D'Andrea's Secret Occult Gallery And Spell Casting Formulary

Spell 11

Success Spell Of The Dragon Kings

To attain success, you invite the Dragon Kings to work with you. Through a combination of various tools, you can attain success in your chosen area, such as: love, protection, lust, money or spirituality.

You need to acquire some cinnamon. This herb is connected to the element of fire. This is the Breath of the Dragon.

This is Power, masculine energy in full force. It is also connected to the radiant energy of the Sun.

To achieve success:
1. Burn cinnamon incense to raise your spiritual vibration. Anoint yourself with a drop of cinnamon oil in the palm of your hand and a drop on your third eye. Focus your intent/purpose while doing so.

2. Next, ask the Dragon Kings to work with you for the purpose of (FILL IN YOUR PURPOSE). Tell them you will honor them by utilizing their oil (as stated above) and burning a white candle (any size- fire) for them. Also, say that when your intent comes in, you will honor them again by burning cinnamon incense and lighting a white candle to thank them.

EXTREMELY IMPORTANT- Do not make this promise lightly. Only if you can carry it through – or your intent will be lost.

Conclusion

There are numerous avenues and byways to reach the same destination.

They all converge down through time from the Ancients to the One Source – to a Divine Being. The name for the One does not matter. The label we utilize is simply to make us able to communicate to each other what we perceive, to the best of our ability.

Through walking on the Path of Light we all come together to elevate our own spiritual level, to aid others to become enlightened and to heal the planet we inhabit.

We are all part of the cycle of life and nature.

Be positive, aware, spiritual, and you will not go wrong. Whatever you do really does come back eventually. Remember, you can't do better than your source. With Divine Power on your side you are virtually unbeatable.

**Maria D'Andrea's Secret Occult Gallery
And Spell Casting Formulary**

About The Author

Rev. Maria D'Andrea was born in Budapest, Hungary. Since early childhood Maria has demonstrated high levels of psychic ability. As an Ordained Minister and pastoral Counselor, Maria has provided excellent psychic guidance and enlightenment to many. She is considered a Spiritual Leader of her time.

A professional psychic and occultist, she is the founder of the Hermetic Order of the Sylvan Society. She is also the founder of the Psi Esoteric Guild and Maria D'Andrea Solomon's Psychic/Metaphysical Programs.

Rev. Maria's psychic abilities and talents for numerous years include Psychic, Rune Casting, Tarot, Biorhythm, Kirlian Photography, Numerology, Trance States, Automatic Writing, Occultism, Card Reading, and Er Mei Chi Gong. She is well known for teaching Principles and Techniques in the psychic and metaphysical fields. She is a certified Hypnotist, holds a Doctor of Metaphysics Degree, D.D., D.R.H., DRS, Principal Teacher of ISA and a Healing Minister.

Rev. Maria has been a guest speaker, lecturer at universities, business forums, metaphysical and parapsychology organizations throughout the country. She has published articles on spiritual and pastoral guidance in numerous magazines and professional journals. She has appeared on radio, TV and cable television shows.

Maria D'Andrea's Secret Occult Gallery And Spell Casting Formulary

Notes

Maria D'Andrea's Secret Occult Gallery
And Spell Casting Formulary

OTHER BOOKS BY MARIA D'ANDREA
That Are Available Only From Her Website
(Including ebook Versions)
www.MariaDAndrea.com

Psychic Vibrations of Crystals, Gems and Stones

The New Age Formulary – A Workbook For Creating A Positive Life

Helping Yourself With Magickal Oils A-Z

Instant Money Empowerment

Do It Yourself Wicca

How To Terminate Stress With Mediation Strategies

Services & Products

Readings, Numerous Classes and Programs, Guided Meditations, Tapes, CDs, DVDs and products available.

email: mdandrea100@gmail.com

Maria D'Andrea's Secret Occult Gallery And Spell Casting Formulary

Maria D'Andrea's Secret Occult Gallery And Spell Casting Formulary

Spell 12

Happiness And Harmony Spell

The scent of fresh basil (herb) causes harmony and empathy between two people, thus making it easier for you to deal with others. They need to be able to smell the herb for this to achieve the proper outcome. This will calm arguments, as well.

Rub the leaves against your skin as a natural perfume

Basil is utilized in love divination by putting two basil leaves on live coal. Look at them as they burn. If they burn to ashes next to each other, the relationship will last. If they burn and crackle, it will not last. In this case, look at the relationship to see what you can do to improve it before it gets to that point.

Placed in a home, it is protection to give you safety and harmony.

As a spell, take three basil leaves, hold them in your hand and say:

By the Power of three times three,
By the Power that is meant to be,
From night to day,
And day to night,
Happiness and harmony are now all mine.

Then take the leaves and place them thus:
1- Put one in your bedroom.
2- Put one in your purse or wallet or anywhere within three feet of your body to carry always.
3- Put one in your car or in the room you spend the most time in.

HERE ARE THE LATEST MYSTICAL SECRETS FROM FAMED HUNGARIAN BORN PSYCHIC MARIA D'ANDREA, REVEALED IN HER NEW BOOK AND VIDEO DRAMATIZATION

TURN AN ORDINARY GLASS OF DRINKING WATER AND AN INEXPENSIVE CRYSTAL INTO A POWERFUL ELIXIR FOR IMPROVED GOOD HEALTH, ENHANCED PSYCHIC ABILITIES AND THE FORTIFICATION OF INNER STRENGTH

Just about everyone has their favorite crystal or gemstone these days. Anyone who believes in the power of nature's most beautiful "gifts from God" realizes that there is power in them there stones. It has been scientifically proven that they can be used as psychic energizers and to greatly enhance one's life and bring about amazing benefits. **The Old Testament**, for example, is rich in references to crystals and gemstones. The breastplate of Aaron was made up of 12 gemstones, including emerald, beryl, topaz, sapphire, agate, onyx, jasper, amethyst, lapis and turquoise. These stones seemingly embraced all of the colors of the spectrum and were used to absorb or repel the radiation emitted from the Ark of the Covenant which had stored up the energy of an atomic bomb.

But do you know how to get the most out of your favorite crystal or gemstone? You can't just hold it in your hand and say abracadabra – you need to know the proper way to energize and enhance the powers that are stored up inside. Maria D'Andrea, Hungarian born psychic and shaman through the pages of her latest book and a video dramatization will teach you how to unlock the enormous vibrations that you have at your very own fingertips with a simple "trick" that includes just using an ordinary glass of tap water.

Maria's **SECRET MAGICKAL ELIXIRS OF LIFE** workbook and DVD study guide kit contains everything you need to know to "pump up the power" of what may seem to be ordinary stones that can be found right outside your door, turning them into highly personal talismans. The importance of a stone's shape is also described as well as what the color of a particular stone signifies. You will even find out the necessity of wearing certain crystals and gems during specific times of the week due to their astrological connections, as ruled by the magnetism of the planets.

MAGICAL STONES

Just about every type of stone has relevance in God's order of things. "Special Blessings" and protections can come to the wearer of a crystal or stone, if worn while repeating certain prayers or performing simple rituals.

Such stones can be utilized when business is bad…when you need to take a purification bath…when you need to receive information about another person…when money is needed…when you wish to attract good luck…find a new friend, or a potential lover.

You will be given specific rituals using stones that the author says can bring you great prosperity…can help in meditation…can promote harmony around you…can strengthen the user spiritually, and can grant all your wishes. There are instructions on how to turn an ordinary glass of tap water into the "Fountain of Youth" with one of the formulas given in this book. And best of all, these "Magickal Stones" need NOT be expensive gems like diamonds or rubies. In most cases, they are ordinary stones which have little – or no – monetary value and which you can easily obtain on your own.

PREDICTING THE FUTURE

Fortune tellers and diviners have always been with us. In addition to various forms of crystals, other stones can also be used to peer into the future. Using Maria's proven methods, the reader will learn how to have prophetic dreams with stones, how to pick up psychic vibrations from other people using crystals and gemstones, and how to see into the future in order to guide and shape your own life, as well as the lives of perfect strangers and those closest to you.

BIRTHSTONES AND WEDDING RINGS

Find out which stones are best suited for you according to your individual birthday and what engagement or wedding ring you should give or receive to enhance the relationship. Maria D'Andrea's **SECRET MAGICKAL ELIXIRS OF LIFE** is guaranteed to add great meaning to your life and is of importance to every person who would like to increase their position in the cosmic arrangement of things.

ORDER NOW!

Your copy of **SECRET MAGICKAL ELIXIRS** book and DVD kit awaits you. To order just send **$25.00 + $5.00** shipping and handling to:

**TIMOTHY G. BECKLEY, BOX 753
NEW BRUNSWICK, NJ 08903**

AMAZING BENEFITS OF GEMSTONES

MARIA'S SECRET MAGICKAL ELIXIRS OF LIFE WILL TELL YOU HOW TO BE ABLE TO EASILY ASCERTAIN WHICH STONES ARE BEST SUITED FOR…

O Healing Purposes;
O Telepathy;
O Strengthening The Aura;
O Attracting A Lover;
O Obtaining Money And Prosperity;
O Controlling The Weather;
O Magnifying Your Desires;
O Shedding All Worries And Anxieties;
O Protection From Negativity;
O Bringing Courage To The Holder;
O Winning A Court Case;
O Use As An Elixir.

ALSO AVAILABLE — SPECIALLY PREPARED GEMSTONE KIT YOU CAN USE WITH MARIA'S BOOKS & DVDS

. This kit contains green agate, amethyst, carnelian, citrine, hematite, green jasper, rose quartz, green quartz, clear quartz, sodalite, and tiger's eye, as well as a vial of lavender oil and a blue bag to carry the kit in when you travel.

**MARIA'S BOOK, DVD AND GEMSTONE KIT —
All items this page just
$45.00 + $7.00 S/H**

OTHER VALUABLE BOOKS BY MARIA D'ANDREA
– ALL LARGE FORMAT WORKBOOKS · EACH INCLUDES A BONUS DVD –

( ) HEAVEN SENT MONEY SPELLS – DIVINELY INSPIRED FOR YOUR WEALTH

Find out why Maria is called "The Money Psychic." Imagine receiving money just by using the powers of your mind. Want a new home? Or pay off an existing mortgage?

Would you like to go on an exotic "dream" vacation with someone who is sexy or your true love? Want to sell the items laying around in your garage or attic for BIG CASH? Interested in picking a large prize lottery ticket, or winning at the tables or slot machines?

Tired of seeing someone else wearing the "Bling?" Diamonds are a girls best friend, but who cares about anyone else when that fabulous stone could be around your finger or neck?

Includes Simple Money Spells DVD— $21.95

Author And Practitioner
Maria D' Andrea

( ) YOUR PERSONAL MEGA POWER SPELLS
Includes Free 60 Minute DVD – "Put A Spell On You 'Cause Your Mine!"

Hundreds of spells that are so powerful their practitioners were once put to death for being witches. Includes spells for protection against unseen forces. Spells for love and romance. Spells for drawing the cornucopia of luck into your life. Spells for creating positive cash flow to enhance your prosperity. Spells for a healthy life. Spells for divining life's purposes with positive magick. Spells for faxing your heart's desires through meditation and visualization. — **$24.00**

EXPLORE THE SPIRITUAL WORLD WITH MARIA - MINI WORKSHOPS AND SEMINARS NOW ON DVD

**Check Off Desired Titles: $10 each – 3 for $22.00 10 for $79.95
All 16 just $99.95**

1. ( ) **Rearrange Your Life With Positive Energy**
2. ( ) **Adventures Of A UFO Tracker With Tim Beckley And Maria**
3. ( ) **The Amazing Power Of Tesla Energy**
4. ( ) **2012 And Beyond – What Can We Expect?**
5. ( ) **Manifesting A New Reality**
6. ( ) **Exploring The Healer Within You**
7. ( ) **Spiritual And Magickal Runes**
8. ( ) **Soul Mind Dreaming**
9. ( ) **Gemstones How They Rock**
10.( ) **Tap To Manifest**
11.( ) **Angels And The Fall**
12.( ) **A Shamanic Life**
13.( ) **Surrender – Effortless Techniques**
14.( ) **The Power Of Planting Positive Seeds**
15.( ) **Attracting A Relationship**
16.( ) **Gemstones And Your Chakras**

Ordering Information: Each Episode Of **Exploring The Spiritual World Of Maria** is approximately 30 minutes in length and are of broadcast quality. Add $5.00 for S/H.

(Because of their low price these DVDs are shipped in sleeves. Cases not included).

( ) OCCULT GRIMOIRE AND MAGICAL FORMULARY

Cover Art by Carol Ann Rodriguez

Ten books in one! – Over 500 spells! Over 200 oversized pages! With the help of this book you will learn: To manifest your own future destiny. To prevent psychic attack. To use herbal magnets. To apply candle magic to receive individual blessings. To unlock secrets of love potions. To mix the best mystical incense. To draw on the powers of crystals and stones. How prayer really works. The only true application for ritualistic oils. — **$25.00**

( ) SPECIAL OFFER OF THESE 3 BOOKS/DVDS BY MARIA — $59.95 + $8 P/H

**ORDER DIRECTLY FROM:
TIMOTHY G. BECKLEY, BOX 753
NEW BRUNSWICK, NJ 08903**

Raymond A. Palmer Tribute Edition

WHAT IS OAHSPE?
THOUSANDS HAVE CALLED IT THE WONDER BOOK OF THE AGES.

Want To Know Just Where Is Heaven? What We Do When We Get There? Is There A Hell? Who "Manages" Earth, the Solar System, the Universe... and How?

OAHSPE reveals all this, and a thousand more answers to man's most difficult questions. Received from spirit in 1880 using one of the first typewriters at the unbelievable speed of 120 words per minute – a miracle in itself. In addition, much of the writing, along with the book's original drawings, was done in total darkness.

PRESENTED IN TWO VOLUMES, 1250 PAGES NEARLY A MILLION WORDS!

To many this work is one of the most astronomical ever presented. It is a book of Cosmology that could have been written by today's space scientists.

Do you think flying saucers are new? Then read OAHSPE! A whole panorama of aerial and special vessels are described as though from today's newspapers.

Do you wonder at Einstein's theories? Then read OAHSPE! He could have gotten his information from these pages!

Uncounted thousands of tons of meteorites fall to Earth each day, yet space is nearly empty of them. OAHSPE knew it in 1882!

Space is dark, say our daring astronauts. So did OAHSPE in 1882, and tells us why!

Archaeologists have claimed amazing discoveries of ancient races and dead cities and civilizations since 1882. They might have discovered them sooner had they read OAHSPE!

THIS EDITION IS DEDICATED TO THE LATE PUBLISHER, EDITOR AND RESEARCHER, RAY PALMER, WHO THOUGHT THIS ONE OF THE GREATEST WORKS EVER PENNED

Special: This is the only edition of OAHSPE to contain FULL COLOR PORTRAITS of the spirits responsible for dictating this amazing work to John Newbrough.
Over 1250 Pages - Two Volume Set - Color Plates - Retail Price $99.00
ISBN13: 9781606110676

PRICE REDUCED FROM $99.00 TO $79.95 FOR READERS OF THIS PUBLICATION ONLY!
Because of weight and size add $8.00 shipping/handling.
Copies shipped directly from the printer.

Order From: TIMOTHY G. BECKLEY · BOX 753 · NEW BRUNSWICK, NJ 08903

FREE DVD WITH ORDERS OF $30 OR MORE - HUNTING FOR BOOGIE MAN & SEARCH FOR THE TRICKSTER

His Powers Are Unsurpassed In The West
T. Lobsang Rampa "Miracle Man"

TWO TITLES NEVER RELEASED IN NORTH AMERICA!
NEW! BEYOND THE TENTH
RAMPA HAS DECLARED...

OVER TEN MILLION BOOKS SOLD WORLDWIDE!

"Man is one tenth conscious, the other nine tenths deal with the subconscious and all that which comes under the heading."

"THIS BOOK IS ABOUT YOU! NOT JUST ABOUT ONE TENTH OF YOU, BUT ALSO THAT WHICH GOES BEYOND THE TENTH"

For many years the famous author and occult master has been asked thousands of questions from both students and admirers from all over the world. They all want to know how they can better their own lives and how they can bring about a global spiritual revolution which would include all of humankind, not just one political group or religious sect.

Every half million years (give or take) the earth sees fit to shuck off its stock, as it goes about preparing the surface of the planet for the next bunch, whom it hopes might be more successful in living in harmony with nature and the cosmic plan.

If you are traumatized by the insanities of our times T. Lobsang Rampa may provide you with some ways to calm your nerves and confront the devils that seek to stifle our every movement and prevent us from becoming the individual we were meant to be.

BEYOND THE TENTH is a rally cry for what is transpiring all around us. Come and join the "party" and free yourself from the manacles of self imposed human slavery.

BEYOND THE TENTH is the favorite work of many Rampa fans. Order now for just **$18.00**

NEW! CANDLELIGHT
ANSWERS ARE FINALLY GIVEN — THE TRUTH ABOUT RAMPA'S TRANSMIGRATION

Cynicism has always been a part of the author's existence. Those that disbelieve who T. Lobsang Rampa says he is will never be convinced otherwise.

Those that believe need to be offered nothing additional in the way of evidence.

In this wonderfully fulfilling work, the great mystic reveals the truth about transmigration and how he went for being an ordinary plumber (or was he?) to one of the most remarkable men in the world of mysticism:

Says Tuesday Lobsang Rampa about this puzzling phenomenon:

"Transmigration is stated to be the movement of one soul from one body into another body. There are many, many recorded instances in the world's history in which the soul of a person has departed from a body but before death occurred to that body another body was taken over. It is as simple as that."

Get ready to be propelled in an out of this world experience. Here are little known facts about reincarnation, including who you were and who you might be in the future. Understanding is the key to expanding your consciousness and opening your heart and mind to the universe. Rampa will guide you.

JUST FOLLOW THE FLICKER OF THE CANDLELIGHT!
For your personal copy of Candlelight just send $18.00

SPECIAL OFFER
BOTH NEW TITLES JUST $32.00 + $5.00 S/H

MORE RAMPA TITLES
Large Format Editions
Check Desired Items -- Just $20 Each

( ) **THE THIRD EYE** - This is the book that started it all back in the 1950s, revealing Rampa's psychic abilities.
( ) **THE HERMIT** - A dark cavern holds great wisdom from the ancients.
( ) **THE RAMPA STORY** - Secrets of the Lama's life revealed to the outside world.
( ) **MY VISIT TO AGHARTA** - Journey to the capitol of the underground at the center of the earth.
( ) **DR FROM LHASA** - Wonders and secrets from the Top Of The World!
( ) **TIBETAN SAGE** - Practical uses of Shamanism and powers of the Monks.
( ) **CAVE OF THE ANCIENTS** - Revealing secrets of ancient space ships, lost civilizations, and anti gravity.
( ) **CHAPTERS OF LIFE** - How to make the most out of "hard times."
( ) **LIVING WITH THE LAMA** - 25 years of a cat who telepathically "talked" with TLP.
( ) **SAFFRON ROBE** - Astral travel adds to life's journey of the soul. Rampa leads the way.
( ) **TIBETAN SAGE** - Return to the Hall of Records and the Cave of the Ancients.
( ) **TWILIGHT** - Hidden chambers beneath the earth explored.
( ) **FLIGHT OF THE PUSSYWILLOW** - Mrs Rampa gives her joyful view of worldy events.

SPECIAL ALL 15 RAMPA BOOKS THIS PAGE $249.00 + $12 S/H

RARE RAMPA MEDITATION AND PRAYER AUDIO CD
This is a one of a kind recording - the only know "record" with Rampa's voice on it. Runs approx 40 minutes. Join in his celebration of life. $12.00

Available Now From:
TIMOTHY G. BECKLEY · BOX 753
NEW BRUNSWICK, NJ 08903
Pay Pal Orders use mrufo8@hotmail.com
Credit Cards 732 602-3407

www.ingramcontent.com/pod-product-compliance
Lightning Source LLC
Chambersburg PA
CBHW081920170426
43200CB00014B/2785